Tell Along Tales!

Tell Along Tales!

Playing with Participation Stories

Dianne de Las Casas

Illustrated by Soleil Lisette

LIBRARIES UNLIMITED

AN IMPRINT OF ABC-CLIO, LLC
Santa Barbara, California • Denver, Colorado • Oxford, England

Library of Congress Cataloging-in-Publication Data

de Las Casas, Dianne.
    Tell along tales! : playing with participation stories / Dianne de Las Casas ; illustrated by Soleil Lisette.
        p. cm.
    Includes bibliographical references and index.
    ISBN 978-1-59884-635-5 (hard copy : acid-free paper) — ISBN 978-1-59884-636-2 (ebook)
1. Children's libraries—Activity programs.   2. Storytelling.   I. Lisette, Soleil.   II. Title.
    Z718.3.D436   2011
    027.62'51—dc22   2011000335

ISBN: 978-1-59884-635-5
EISBN: 978-1-59884-636-2

15   14   13   12   11   1   2   3   4   5

This book is also available on the World Wide Web as an eBook.
Visit www.abc-clio.com for details.

Libraries Unlimited
An Imprint of ABC-CLIO, LLC

ABC-CLIO, LLC
130 Cremona Drive, P.O. Box 1911
Santa Barbara, California 93116-1911

This book is printed on acid-free paper ∞

Manufactured in the United States of America

Contents

Stories

Introduction

I love connecting with my audience in a special way. For me, that way has been audience participation. It's so much fun to see the audience singing, chanting, clapping, rapping, wiggling, and giggling. I love it when stories are interactive, fully involving the audience.

Storytelling is, inherently, an active listening experience. Audiences don't just hear and watch; they listen and experience. Unlike theater, there is no fourth wall in storytelling. The storyteller looks into the audience's eyes, engaging them in the tale. Audience participation takes the active listening experience to another level. Together, the storyteller and the audience co-create the tale, adding sound effects, songs, chants, call and response, or other audience participation techniques. It is a fun way to connect with audiences of all ages.

I have been doing "tell along tales" for many years now. The difference between a good tell along tale and a great tell along tales is audience management! Pay special attention to settle-downs. When you bring an audience up, you must be able to bring them back down. Experiment, modify the tales, and give the stories your own flair. You'll enjoy the reaction of your audience when you twist tales with participation. Most of all, have fun!

So play with participation and have your audience tell along!

Warmly,
Dianne de Las Casas
dianne@storyconnection.net
http://www.storyconnection.net

Chapter 1
How to Tell a Story

The Definition of Storytelling

According to the National Council for Teachers of English, as written in their Position Statement from the Committee on Storytelling, the definition of storytelling is as follows:

Storytelling is relating a tale to one or more listeners through voice and gesture. It is not the same as reading a story aloud or reciting a piece from memory or acting out a drama—though it shares common characteristics with these arts. The storyteller looks into the eyes of the audience and together they compose the tale. The storyteller begins to see and re-create, through voice and gesture, a series of mental images; the audience, from the first moment of listening, squints, stares, smiles, leans forward or falls asleep, letting the teller know whether to slow down, speed up, elaborate, or just finish. Each listener, as well as each teller, actually composes a unique set of story images derived from meanings associated with words, gestures, and sounds. The experience can be profound, exercising the thinking and touching the emotions of both teller and listener.

The above description is the most thorough and eloquent definition. It needs no further elaboration.

Why Storytelling Is a Vital Art Form

Storytelling engages the listener in whole brain activity. Both the logical and creative sides of the mind are utilized when listening to a story. In addition, storytelling does the following:

- Encourages appreciation of language and literature
- Demonstrates values
- Promotes literacy
- Teaches communication and social skills
- Celebrates cultural diversity
- Preserves history
- Inspires creativity
- Engages the imagination

Through the oral tradition, we preserve the past and help shape the future.

Where to Find Stories

Stories are everywhere! You can find them in the following.

Your Imagination

Many storytellers like to tell original stories, tales that they have personally created. Sometimes, the details of a story can become fuzzy over time, especially if you have not told the story in some time. Be sure to write the story down or, at the very least, create a written outline.

Your Family History

Every family has interesting stories. My great grandfather possessed a wicked sense of humor. He named my grandfather James O. James Sr. My grandfather carried on his sense of humor and named my father James O. James Jr. As you can imagine, many stories have arisen out of the adventures my grandfather and father had with their "first-name-is-their-last-name-is-their-first-name" scenario. Think back and recall your childhood—do you remember any family stories? Interview your family members for stories. You are bound to have a treasure chest of family story gems at your fingertips.

Your Personal History

Many of us have led interesting lives. Donald Davis's strength is in retelling personal and family stories. He has made an art and a living of it. His family stories are filled with universal truths that speak to each of his audiences. When looking at your own life as a source for stories, find the lesson you learned from that chapter in your life. Perhaps that lesson can serve as the foundation for a story that will touch your audiences.

Fairy Tales, Folklore, Myths, and Legends

Because of my childhood life overseas, I am drawn to stories from around the world, particularly stories from this genre. I love researching stories from other cultures. A great place to start is your local library. Visit the 398.2 section, where you will find folklore.

For more in-depth research on folklore, use Margaret Read MacDonald's 1982 edition of *The Storyteller's Sourcebook*. Margaret Read MacDonald says, "The eleven years spent compiling this index were a part of my folklore Ph.D. work. The book indexes 556 folktale collections and 389 folktale picture books. The book is arranged according to the Stith Thompson motif-index classification used by folklorists. But most users simply look up their tale under the title or subject index. It's a fun book to browse." A 2002 supplement to *The Storyteller's Sourcebook* has been released, covering folklore collections and picture books from 1983 through 1999.

Literary Stories

Retelling literature from such notable authors as Edgar Allen Poe, Rudyard Kipling, and O. Henry would fall under this category. If you decide to retell literary stories, you must utilize stories that are in the public domain. Otherwise, you will need to obtain permission from the author or publishing house that maintains the copyright on the work you wish to use.

Historical Accounts

If you are fascinated with history, retellings of historical accounts may be just the genre for you. When you retell stories based on historical facts, accuracy and research of the facts is imperative.

The Internet

The Internet is a story buffet! Stories from virtually every culture can be found on the Internet. I use Google as my search engine, and I find a plethora of stories at my fingertips.

How to Shape Stories

Shaping stories for telling and retelling follow three basic principles:

1. Build the story around a good plot.

2. Create characters that audiences will care about.

3. Good dialogue moves the story along.

Crafting the tellable story is an art. Written stories often need to be recrafted because the language is not suited to the oral tradition. What looks good on paper does not necessarily sound good to the listening audience. When telling a story orally, many dialogue introductions, such as "He said" and "She said" may be dropped because the teller is conveying that through body language and vocal characterization.

Storytelling is often less formal than written language, even conversational in style. There are, of course, times when a more formal presentation of a story is appropriate, such as with literary stories or period pieces. Individual stories will differ. A "Brer Rabbit" tale will engage audiences with the loose, conversational style of the South, while the tale of "Annabel Lee" by Edgar Allen Poe will need to retain its archaic language and structure.

Learning Stories

To learn a story, you must first live with the story. If you are learning a story from a printed version, read and reread the story several times. If you are crafting an original tale or a story from an oral source, it helps to write down the outline of the story line. The story should become a part of you so that when you open your mouth to tell the story, the words magically fall from your lips. Kendall Haven, a renowned storyteller and author, says, "There are two parts to the word storytelling: 'story' and 'telling.' Beginning tellers often focus just on the telling part and forget to spend enough time understanding and learning the story so well that they could tell it naturally as if it had really happened to them."

Many beginning tellers make the mistake of trying to memorize a story word for word. This creates a problem when you are in the middle of telling the story and you struggle to remember the exact words. When this happens, you end up losing your place entirely, forgetting the story. There are several ways to learn a story without memorizing it. Storytellers of national reputation build repertoires of hundreds of stories by practicing one or more of the following techniques.

Memorize Your Opening Line

Without memorizing the entire story, make the opening line significant and remember it.

Outline the Story

Write down the bare bones of the story from beginning to end.

Create a Storyboard

If you are a visual learner, draw your stories out, scene by scene, like a cartoon. A great example of a storyboard can be found at the Eduplace.com website at http://www.eduplace.com/rdg/gen_act/pigs/story_mp.html.

Visualize the Story

Like a director directing a play, you are the director of the theater of your mind. Visualize how the story takes place in your imagination. Use words that describe what you are seeing.

Type the Story

If you are a visual/tactile learner, you may enjoy learning stories by absorbing them and then retyping them.

Listen to the Story

If you are an aural learner, record the story onto a voice recorder and listen to it. Many of today's cell phones are even equipped with voice recorders that can then be synced to your computer! Take advantage of technology.

Fill in the Details

After you have learned the bones of your story, fill in the details using the visual pictures that you have created in your mind.

Memorize Repeating Refrains

With audience participation, there is often a repeating refrain. These lines should be memorized so that you can deliver them consistently, fulfilling the audience's expectations.

Memorize Your Last Line

To give dramatic punch to your story, create a significant ending line that ties the pieces of your story together.

Keep Good Source Notes

It is always a good idea to keep track of the sources from where your stories originated. Sometimes, a storyteller needs to access their research to fill in story details or add participation elements to the tale.

If you are telling a traditional folktale, you may want to incorporate a traditional folktale beginning and ending. A great list of folktale openings and closings can be found in Tim and Leanne Jennings's "Folktale Openings and Closings" at http://www.folktale.net.

Chapter 2
Audience Participation

As you gain experience as a storyteller, it's fun to add audience participation stories to your repertoire, especially if you work with children. Audience participation, which is when the audience joins in your telling, can be fun and exciting. It's a great way to involve and interact with your audience. When you play with your stories, your audience will play with you.

Various Types of Audience Participation

Call and Response

Call and response is when the storyteller calls out a word or phrase and the audience responds with an answer.

Rehearsed Response

Some audience participation is best taught before the story begins, particularly if the participation is more complicated (i.e., with a refrain and hand motions).

Directed Role Playing

This involves soliciting volunteers from the audience and directing them as a character in the story. Keep their participation simple so as not to distract from the story. For example, when I tell my story *The Gigantic Sweet Potato* (Pelican Publishing, 2010), I have audience members help me pull up the gigantic sweet potato. It's fun, and the role players and the audience enjoy it.

Audience Query

Audience query is when the storyteller asks a question to elicit an answer from the audience. It is best used when the storyteller knows exactly what the audience will answer. For example, in a spooky story, the storyteller asks, "Do you think he should open the door?" Most of the audience members will answer with a vehement "No!"

Dramatic Pause

Dramatic pause is when you add a pregnant pause during a point in your story and the audience "fills in the blank" automatically. A good example of this is when the storyteller rubs her belly and says, "He was getting really . . ." [*Pause*], and the audience chimes in, "hungry!" I like to use the dramatic pause to fill in a predictable blank.

Spontaneous Joining In

Spontaneous joining in often occurs when there are repeating refrains, songs, and well-placed dramatic pauses. A good audience participation story usually elicits spontaneous joining in.

Combinations of the Various Types of Audience Participation

A story does not have to be restricted to one type of audience participation technique. An experienced storyteller can have multiple elements of audience participation in one story.

Vehicles to Encourage Audience Participation

Repeating Chants

Teach a chant that you use throughout your story and have your audience join in, saying it with you.

Repeating Songs

Like the chant, a song can be used throughout the story with your audience singing with you each time the song appears in the story. Like a chorus in a song, the audience becomes familiar with the repetition and joins in.

Sounds

Stories with sounds such as rain (snapping of fingers) and thunder (stomping of feet) can be used as vehicles for audience participation. Rhythm instruments are great ways to create sounds within stories too.

Movement

If your story has repetitive action, the use of movement can be an effective vehicle for audience participation. In the story, "Going on a Bear Hunt," I say "We can't go over it," and we (the audience and I) motion "over" with our two arms arched above our heads, like a bridge. When I say, "We can't go under it," we motion "under" by kneeling and putting our arms straight in front of us, close to the ground.

Dramatization

Dramatizing a character so that the character maintains that particular characterization throughout the story often encourages audiences to become that same character with their bodies and faces. For example, young children will often mirror the storyteller. If the storyteller is a bear in the story, the children will dramatize the character with their faces and their bodies, even without prompting.

Dramatic Pause

Tell the story to a certain point and pause dramatically, waiting for the audience to chime in and fill in the blank. As I said before, it is best used when the audience's answer is predictable.

Elements in a Story That Provide Opportunity for Participation

Here are some other elements that provide great opportunity for you to add participation to your story:

- Sounds (wind, footsteps, knocking, creaking doors, etc.)
- Animals (growling, squeaking, slithering, stomping, etc.)

- Repetitive action
- Repeating phrases
- Characters interacting with each other

When to Include Audience Participation

Audience participation can be used at any time, but it is best not to tell audience participation stories when it is the children's naptime or when they are hungry. This applies especially to preschool and kindergarten students. Audience participation works well in these situations:

- After the audience is "warmed up"
- In the middle of a storytelling program
- With grades K–5
- With mixed crowds of kids and adults (family programs)

How to Choose and Coach Kids for Directed Role Playing

Survey the audience to see who is actively listening and enjoying your program. Ask for volunteers and choose kids who raise their hands quietly and are not jumping up and down trying to get your attention or saying, "Me! Me! Me!" Be succinct with your instructions (i.e., "The lion was taking a nap." [*Whispering into participant's ear "close your eyes"*]). Have fun with them!

Other Audience Participation Techniques

Once you have told a few audience participation stories, it becomes a lot easier. Here are some other participation techniques:

- A sing-along is a good way to warm audience up.
- Use poetry with repeating lines.

- Rhythm instruments are a great way to encourage and incorporate audience participation. I love using rhythm instruments from around the world. Creative Diversity is a great company that has "multicultural products for early childhood." I love their basket of instruments from around the globe.

- Use the rule of "3 to 5"—stories that have repetitive action in it at least three to five times usually make great audience participation stories. Think "Three Little Pigs" ("I'll huff and I'll puff and I'll blow your house down!"), "Goldilocks," and other traditional folktales and fairy tales.

Chapter 3
Audience Management

Imagine walking into an auditorium (gym or "cafetorium") filled with 400 wiggly, overly energetic, boisterous students who are being yelled at by their teachers to "settle down" or "shut up." Imagine that it is in the afternoon right after lunch and the air-conditioning isn't working properly. It is 90 degrees outside, so they have the door propped open. Now all the outside cacophony pollutes your performance space, and a large fan is turned to high, making a loud whirring sound that could drown out a 747's engine. How do you manage an audience in these types of conditions or worse?

The above scenario is not imagined. It actually happened to me, and it could happen to you. At some point or another, as storytellers, we will face the inevitability of audience management in less-than-desirable conditions. In a performance, it is a storyteller's responsibility to (1) manage the audience, (2) connect with the audience, and (3) connect with the story. Audience management is a skill that is honed over time with performance experience. It is a must when you are telling audience participation stories. Here are a few tips.

Spot Potential Problems before the Program Begins

Before the program, survey your audience. Look for children that are overly energetic or misbehaving. Approach them before the show and ask them to be "role models" for the other children. They usually respond positively. At the end of the program, acknowledge their good behavior. This helps to eliminate potential behavioral problems during the performance.

Take Care of "Housekeeping" in the Beginning

If you are telling to a family audience in a public venue, take care of housekeeping before the show begins. You or someone in charge should remind the audience of the following:

- Where the restrooms are located
- To turn off their electronic devices
- To take small children out of the performance area if they need a "break"

Use Sound Reinforcement

If you are telling to a group larger than 50 or 75, I highly recommend using a sound system. Taking care of your audience means responding to their needs. In order for your audience to connect to you and your story, they need to be able to hear the storytelling clearly. Sound reinforcement also helps you by decreasing voice strain.

Warmly Welcome Your Audience

Welcome your audience and let them know how much you appreciate their participation in the program. A warm welcome will set the tone for the rest of the program.

Set Audience Expectations

Let your audience know what you expect of them. If you want them to sing along or participate in a story, coach them and help them practice their lines or chorus. If they are too loud or boisterous in their participation, use positive reinforcement and let them know that you appreciate their enthusiasm but explain the difference between using an "indoor" voice and an "outdoor" voice or a "big" voice and a "small" voice.

Select Age-Appropriate Stories

The fastest way to lose an audience is to select stories that are not age appropriate. For example, telling a 25-minute story with no audience participation to a group of preschoolers will not work. They will quickly lose interest after the first five minutes. Choose stories that work with your audience and pace your program accordingly. A more appropriate selection for preschoolers would be short stories with repetitive audience participation and fast-paced story bridges such as fingerplays and songs between stories.

Articulate Clear Instructions

If you are requesting audience participation or volunteers, provide concise and complete instructions. If your audience does not understand what you are requesting, they will be confused and lose interest.

Maintain Eye Contact

Contact is vital to storytelling. It is the connection between you, your audience, and the story. When telling to large groups, make eye contact with the group as a whole, especially those audience members located in the back. They are usually the first to lose interest because they are farther away. Do not let your eyes rest on someone for more than three seconds. This could cause uneasiness in the audience member. Eye contact allows you to respond to your audience's reaction to the story and vice versa.

Regain Control if a Distraction Occurs

There will be times when the inevitable occurs: a siren screams in the middle of a story, a bell rings as you are telling, or a bug crawls in front of the kids and they find it more interesting to play with than listening to a story. If a distraction occurs, pause long enough to either let the distraction finish or eliminate the distraction (and I don't mean squash the bug). Refocus and continue your story (i.e., "As I was saying, when the queen found out that her pig was stolen . . .").

Warm-Ups, Keep-Ups, and Settle-Downs

Warm-ups and keep-ups are short stretchers, songs, games, chants, or poems that help warm up an audience and keep their energy level up for the duration of the program. They can also help transition from one story to another, acting as a bridge between story activities. I like to think of warm-ups and keep-ups as the glue that holds a storytelling program together. Some of my favorites are in *Crazy Gibberish and Other Story Stretchers* and *Storytime Stretchers* by Naomi Baltuck. Her books are invaluable resources for the storyteller.

Sometimes, boisterous audience participation can cause audiences to become overly enthusiastic and excited. If this happens, use fun ways to settle the audience down. Children automatically shut down when authority figures tell them to "be quiet," "hush up," or "shut up." It is not an effective way to deal with overexcited kids. I created settle-downs to help calm an excited audience. They also work as great transitions between stories and at the end of story programs. I have found that the settle-downs even work to regain control in the classroom. Many schools have their own techniques, such as one finger over the lips and one hand raised in the air or echo clapping, where the teacher claps and the students mirror the pattern. While these techniques are successful in many schools, the settle-downs in this book require no advance coaching and work in any setting with children.

Be Assertive in Taking Appropriate Action

When dealing with hecklers, I usually ignore the first incident. Sometimes, it is just a burst of energy that works itself out. If an incident occurs a second time, I continue with my story but give a stern look to the audience member who is causing the disturbance, letting him/her know that I can see them and know what he/she is doing. This usually stops the disturbance. In extreme cases, I have stopped and firmly confronted the heckler myself or asked an authority figure (grown-up) to administer appropriate action if the heckler continues the behavior. Be assertive and firm. Their disturbance not only interrupts the story but also deprives the other audience members of their right to enjoy the performance.

Praise Your Audience

Praise your audience and thank them for a job well done. Audiences, like performers, want to know when they are doing a good job. I like to say, "Give yourselves a hand for being such a great audience," and clap for them.

Stay Focused

As storytellers, we want to spread the joy of storytelling in as many places as possible, but there are many challenging venues in which to tell stories. Sometimes this means that conditions are less than favorable, and our audience management skills are greatly challenged and put to the test. Stay focused and centered. Remember the significance of the story you are telling.

Audience management is an acquired skill that develops with time. Keep telling whenever and wherever you can, and your audience management skills will increase.

Play with Participation!

Have fun with your stories. Don't be afraid to rework traditional stories, add your own brand of participation, and give the tales your own flair. Use this book as a jumping-off point to explore your own potential to create fun audience participation stories. Soon, you'll have your own original repertoire of Tell Along Tales!

Chapter 4
Warm-Ups and Keep-Ups

How Funky Is Your Chicken?—Original Audience Participation Song

Note from Dianne: *This is such a fun song. Don't be afraid to be inventive and come up with your own animals. You can be really brave and solicit suggestions from the audience. Be prepared to come up with a motion on the spot for a wacky animal you never thought of!*

Audience: Grades PK–5, Ages 4–11

How funky is your chicken? [*Flap elbows like a chicken*]
[*Audience repeats*] How funky is your chicken?
How loose is your goose? [*Wiggle hips*]
[*Audience repeats*] How loose is your goose?

Quacky—Duck [*Open and close one hand to symbolize duck quacking*]

Snappy—Turtle [*Snap fingers*]

Stompin'—Elephant [*Stomp feet*]

Fierce—Lion [*Roar and make claws with both hands*]

Gallopy—Horse [*Gallop hands on lap like a horse*]

Nutty—Squirrel [*Twirl fingers by head as in "crazy"*]

Slitherin'—Snake [*Make waving motion with one hand and arm, like slithering*]

Swingin'—Monkey [*Swing both arms from side to side*]

Jackie Rabbit—Original Adaptation

Note from Dianne: *This story chant was inspired by Dolores Henderson, a Louisiana storyteller, who told me about a little trickster rabbit named Jackie. It's a lot of fun and full of rollicking rhythm.*

Jackie Rabbit [*Storyteller and audience: rabbit X 3*]
Had a habit [*Storyteller and audience: habit X 3*]
Of eatin' cabbage [*Storyteller and audience: cabbage X 3*]
In the garden [*Storyteller and audience: garden X 3*]

Now Mr. Farmer [*Storyteller and audience: farmer X 3*]
Saw Jackie Rabbit [*Storyteller and audience: rabbit X 3*]
Eatin' cabbage [*Storyteller and audience: cabbage X 3*]
In the garden [*Storyteller and audience: garden X 3*]

So Mr. Farmer yelled STOP [*Pause*]
And Jackie ran [*Storyteller and audience: ran X 3*]
To Mama's house [*Storyteller and audience: house X 3*]
Lickety split [*Storyteller and audience: split X 3*]

So now you know [*Storyteller and audience: know X 3*]
Where mischief goes [*Storyteller and audience: goes X 3*]
Trouble follows [*Storyteller and audience: follows X 3*]
Lickety split [*Storyteller and audience: split X 3*]

Don't be that rabbit [*Storyteller and audience: rabbit X 3*]
Eatin' cabbage [*Storyteller and audience: cabbage X 3*]
In the garden [*Storyteller and audience: garden X 3*]
Of Mr. Farmer [*Storyteller and audience: farmer X 3*]

Just be aware [*Storyteller and audience: ware X 3*]
Stay out of trouble [*Storyteller and audience: trouble X 3*]
And be good [*Storyteller and audience: good X 3*]
Lickety split [*Storyteller and audience: split X 3*]

Lickety split [*Storyteller and audience: split X 3 softer*]
Lickety split [*Storyteller and audience: split X 3 and fade out*]

My Aunt Came Back—A Traditional Audience Participation Song

Note from Dianne: Each line and motion is repeated by the audience; continue doing previous motions as you add motions. This is a great song to do in the middle of a story program.

Audience: Grades 2–6, Ages 7–12

My Aunt came back
From old Japan
And brought with her
A paper fan [*Fan self with one hand*]

My Aunt came back
From Old Algiers
And brought with her
A pairs of shears [*Make scissor opening and closing motions with other hand*]

My Aunt came back
From the county fair
And brought with her
A rocking chair [*Rock body back and forth*]

My Aunt came back
From Niagara Falls
And brought with her
Some ping pong balls [*Bop head from side to side*]

My Aunt came back
From Madison
And brought with her
Some chewing gum [*Smack mouth like chewing and sing rest of song like mouth is full*]

My Aunt came back
From Timbuktu

And brought with her [*Slight pause*]
Some nuts like you [*Point to audience. There will be lots of laughter.*]

Onomatopoeia—Original Literacy Game

Note from Dianne: *Discuss onomatopoeia and give examples. Have the students come up with examples of their own. Once they are familiar with the concept, play the game. Everyone stands or sits in a circle. The group chants the chorus. Each player adds a new onomatopoeia word to the chant while repeating the cumulative list. Each player who cannot successfully repeat the cumulative list has to sit in the middle. The circle becomes smaller until there are two people left. Then the entire group gets to snap, clap, and tap for the winners.*

Audience: Grades 4–6, Ages 9–12

Chorus:

Onomatopoeia
Onomatopoeia
Onomatopoeia
Snap, Clap, Tap

Onomatopoeia
Onomatopoeia
Onomatopoeia
First player: Snap, Clap, Tap, [*First player adds*] Bang . . .

Onomatopoeia
Onomatopoeia
Onomatopoeia
Second player: Snap, Clap, Tap, Bang, [*Second player adds*] Boom . . .

Onomatopoeia
Onomatopoeia
Onomatopoeia
Third player: Snap, Clap, Tap, Bang, Boom, [*Third player adds*] Zip . . .

Onomatopoeia
Onomatopoeia
Onomatopoeia
Fourth player: Snap, Clap, Tap, Bang, Boom, Zip, [*Fourth player adds*] Crash . . . etc.

Peanut Butter and Jelly Jam—Original Adaptation

Note from Dianne: This is one of my most popular "keep-ups" or story stretchers. You can watch a video of me performing "Peanut Butter and Jelly Jam" on my website at http://www. storyconnection.net. Click on "Press Kit" and "Videos." You can also find an audio version of it on iTunes from my Jump, Jiggle & Jam *CD.*

Audience: Grades 1–5, Ages 6–11

I got some bread [*Put one hand out in front of you, palm facing up*]
And then I spread [*Clap your other hand on top of your open palm. Flip your hand so the top claps on the palm, then flip your hand again and clap it, palm on palm, one more time. The motion goes with "then I spread."*]
My

Peanut, peanut butter [*Audience says, "And jelly jam." Snap fingers from side to side in front of you with audience doing the same.*]
Peanut, peanut butter [*Audience says, "And jelly jam." Snap fingers from side to side in front of you with audience doing the same.*]

I got some bread [*Put one hand out in front of you, palm facing up.*]
And then I spread [*Clap your other hand on top of your open palm. Flip your hand so the top claps on the palm then flip your hand again and clap it, palm on palm, one more time. The motion goes with "then I spread."*]
My

Apples and bananas [*Audience says, "And jelly jam." With palms facing audience in front of you, move hands from side. Audience will do the same.*]
Peanut, peanut butter [*Audience says, "And jelly jam." Snap fingers from side to side in front of you with audience doing the same.*]

I got some bread [*Put one hand out in front of you, palm facing up*]
And then I spread [*Clap your other hand on top of your open palm. Flip your hand so the top claps on the palm then flip your hand again and clap it, palm on palm, one more time. The motion goes with "then I spread."*]
My

Peppers and pickles [*Audience says, "And jelly jam." With pointer fingers pointing to the ceiling, move them up and down. Audience will do the same.*]
Apples and bananas [*Audience says, "And jelly jam." With palms facing audience in front of you, move hands from side. Audience will do the same.*]

Peanut, peanut butter [*Audience says, "And jelly jam." Snap fingers from side to side in front of you with audience doing the same.*]

I got some bread [*Put one hand out in front of you, palm facing up*]
And then I spread [*Clap your other hand on top of your open palm. Flip your hand so the top claps on the palm, then flip your hand again and clap it, palm on palm, one more time. The motion goes with "then I spread."*]
My

Ketchup and mustard [*Audience says, "And jelly jam." Do the twist. Audience will do the same.*]
Peppers and pickles [*Audience says, "And jelly jam." With pointer fingers pointing to the ceiling, move them up and down. Audience will do the same.*]
Apples and bananas [*Audience says, "And jelly jam." With palms facing audience in front of you, move hands from side. Audience will do the same.*]
Peanut, peanut butter [*Audience says, "And jelly jam." Snap fingers from side to side in front of you with audience doing the same.*]

I got some bread [*Put one hand out in front of you, palm facing up*]
And then I spread [*Clap your other hand on top of your open palm. Flip your hand so the top claps on the palm then flip your hand again and clap it, palm on palm, one more time. The motion goes with "then I spread."*]
My

Sardines and anchovies [*Audience will not say, "And jelly jam." They will say, "Ewwww!" and be totally grossed out. Tell them they have to finish making this gourmet PB&J sandwich. Start with "Sardines and anchovies" again. You are going to make a fish motion. Place both hands in front of you, palms facing down, thumbs out. Put one hand on top of the other and wiggle the thumbs. Instruct the audience to do the same.*]
Ketchup and mustard [*Audience says, "And jelly jam." Do the twist. Audience will do the same.*]
Peppers and pickles [*Audience says, "And jelly jam." With pointer fingers pointing to the ceiling, move them up and down. Audience will do the same.*]
Apples and bananas [*Audience says, "And jelly jam." With palms facing audience in front of you, move hands from side. Audience will do the same.*]
Peanut, peanut butter [*Audience says, "And jelly jam." Snap fingers from side to side in front of you with audience doing the same.*]

I got some bread [*Put one hand out in front of you, palm facing up.*]
My brother said . . .
EWW! Gross! Yuck! Who would eat a sandwich like that?

I grinned at my brother and said, "Brother, I made it for you!" [*Put both hands in front of you as though you are offering a plate. The kids will laugh because many have siblings. I usually ask them if they have a brother or sister they would like to serve that sandwich too. Even grown-ups raise their hands!*]

Pile It on the Pie a Mile High—Original Story Game

Note from Dianne: This game needs no materials other than your imagination. It's a round. It can be played with two people or as many people as you'd like. Everyone adds a "topping" to the top of the pie and has to remember the previous toppings piled on the pie. It can be appetizing and delicious or disgusting and fun. Everybody chants as the game progresses. As the toppings become more bizarre, everyone laughs and makes it difficult to remember all the ingredients. You'll catch on. This is a great way to warm up an audience. Children love giving suggestions and totally lose their inhibitions.

Audience: Grades 3–6, Ages 8–12

Pile it on the pie a mile high
Pile it on the pie a mile high
[*Call a name out*] Eliana!
[*Eliana adds a topping*] Whipped Cream!

Whipped cream on the pie a mile high
Pile it on the pie a mile high
[*Call a name out*] Soleil!
[*Soleil adds a topping*] Nuts!

Nuts and whipped cream
Whipped cream on the pie a mile high
Pile it on the pie a mile high
[*Call a name out*] Dianne!
[*Dianne adds a topping*] Pickles!

Pickles and nuts
Nuts and whipped cream
Whipped cream on the pie a mile high
Pile it on the pie a mile high

[*Call a name out*] Antonio!
[*Antonio adds a topping*] Tuna!

Tuna and pickles
Pickles and nuts
Nuts and whipped cream
Whipped cream on the pie a mile high
Pile it on the pie a mile high . . .

Note from Dianne: This goes on until the group leader (the one who started the game) decides the pie is done. Once the pie is done, yell, "STOP! Uh oh! I feel sick!" Make a wretching sound and then pretend to gag or throw up on one of the players. It's fun to watch everyone scramble. Alternately, you can also say, "STOP! The pie is done. A piece for anyone?" Usually, the kids will respond, "Eeewww! Gross!" or they'll eagerly eat the imaginary pie. When the game is done, the kids usually ask for it again. In addition to being fun, it tests their sequencing skills and ability to recall. So pile it on the pie a mile high!

Ride the Rhyming Pony — An Original Story Stretcher

Note from Dianne: Players are standing in a circle. All the players sing the chorus while clapping their hands on their knees like galloping horses. The first player picks a person and stands in front of them and says a word. The second player has to say a rhyming word in response. All players say the following while clapping hands on knees like a galloping horse:

Ride the rhyming pony, pony
Ride the rhyming pony, pony
Ride the rhyming pony, pony
This is how we do it

Audience: Grades 2–5, Ages 7–11

Chorus:

Ride the rhyming pony, pony
Ride the rhyming pony, pony
Ride the rhyming pony, pony
This is how we do it

First player: [*Picks a person and stands in front of them; says a word (cat)*]
Second player: [*Gives a rhyming word (sat)*] then says:

Sat to the front [*Hop to the front*]
Sat to the side [*Hop to the side*]
Sat to the back [*Hop to the back*]
Come on, let's ride

Chorus:

Ride the rhyming pony, pony
Ride the rhyming pony, pony
Ride the rhyming pony, pony
This is how we do it

Second player: [*Picks a person and stands in front of them; says a word (mat)*]
Third player: [*Gives a rhyming word (bat)*] then says:

Bat to the front [*Hop to the front*]
Bat to the side [*Hop to the side*]
Bat to the back [*Hop to the back*]
Come on, let's ride

Chorus:

Ride the rhyming pony, pony
Ride the rhyming pony, pony
Ride the rhyming pony, pony
This is how we do it

Third player: [*Picks a person and stands in front of them; says a word (pat)*]
Fourth player: [*Gives a rhyming word (chat)*] then says:

Chat to the front [*Hop to the front*]
Chat to the side [*Hop to the side*]
Chat to the back [*Hop to the back*]
Come on, let's ride

Chapter 5
Settle-Downs

With all of these "settle-downs," the children should participate with the storyteller.

Audience: Grades PK–6, Ages 4–12

5 Finger Clap

5 finger clap [*Clap four times with five fingers on each hand*]
4 finger clap [*Clap four times with four fingers on each hand*]
3 finger clap [*Clap four times with three fingers on each hand*]
2 finger clap [*Clap four times with two fingers on each hand*]
1 finger clap [*Clap four times with one finger on each hand*]
Now hands in your lap [*Place hands in your lap*]

Hands on Your Head

Hands on your head [*Put two hands on your head*]
Hands on your hips [*Put hands on each hip*]
Hands out in front [*Hold hands out in front*]
Now finger on the lips [*Put your finger over your lips*]

Head, Shoulders, Tummy, Knees

Head [*Place hands on head*]
Shoulders [*Place hands on shoulders*]

Tummy [*Place hands on stomach*]
Knees [*Place hands on knees*]
Note: Repeat above X4 starting loud and getting quieter each time until your voice is very low. Then say,
Now hands in your lap, please [*Place hands in your lap*]

If You Can Hear Me . . .

If you can hear me, clap your hands once [*Clap one time*]
If you can hear me, clap your hands twice [*Clap two times*]
If you can hear me, clap your hands three times [*Clap three times*]
Now raise your hands in the air and clap [*Hold hands over head and clap one time*]
Now keep your hands together and place them in your lap [*Fold hands together and place in lap*]

Look to the North

Look to the north [*Point and look up*]
Look to the south [*Point and look down*]
Look straight ahead [*Point and look straight ahead*]
Now close our mouths [*Put your finger over your lips*]

Right Hand Up

Right hand up [*Raise your left hand because children will mirror you*]
Right hand down [*Put your left hand down at your side*]
Left hand up [*Raise your right hand because children will mirror you*]
Left hand down [*Put your right hand down at your side*]
Hands in the front [*Hold both hands in front of you*]
Hands in the back [*Hold both hands behind your back*]
Hands to the side [*Hold both hands out, arms raised, at your sides*]
Now hands in your lap [*Place both hands in your lap*]

Shake Your Hands

Shake your hands to the left [*Shake hands to the left*]
Shake your hands to the right [*Shake hands to the right*]
Shake your hands down low [*Shake hands by your knees*]
Shake your hands up high [*Shake hands above your head*]
Shake your hands out in front [*Shake hands in front of you*]

Shake your hands behind your back [*Shake hands behind you*]
Shake your hands everywhere [*Shake hands everywhere*]
Now shake them, shake them, shake them into your lap [*Whisper softer each time to say "shake them" and shake hands slowly to your lap*]

Wave Your Fingers

Note from Dianne: *This is best to settle your audience down when your program is done. I first learned this from storyteller Karen Chace and have since modified it. It always gets some great laughs and is a great way to end a program.*

Wave your fingers [*Wiggle fingers in front of you*]
Wave your toes [*Wiggle your toes*]
Wave your ears [*Wiggle both ears with your hands*]
Wave your nose [*Wiggle your nose with one finger*]
Wave your elbows [*Make a flapping motion with both elbows*]
Wave your hair, if you have any [*Grab your hair with both hands and wave it around*]
Wave your hips [*Wiggle hips from side to side*]
Wave your derriere [*Turn around so that you are shaking your fanny to your audience — this elicits tons of laughter*]
Wave your tongue [*Stick your tongue out and wiggle it around*]
Wave one eye [*Wink one eye*]
Now raise one hand [*Raise one hand*]
And wave good-bye [*Wave good-bye to your audience*]

Stories

Anansi Shares Wisdom with the World

St. Lucia

Note from Dianne: *This story is great for both audience participation, with its repeating story chorus and directed role playing. I like bringing people from the audience to play the owl, the monkey, and the lion. It adds a fun dynamic to the story. I also like using an African shekere, a gourd covered with a net of beads or shells. Since there is a gourd in this story, it goes well with the tale.*

Audience: Grades 1–6, Ages 6–12

Tell along Techniques:

- Repeating chant/song
- Dramatic pause
- Directed role playing
- Movement
- Instruments

Anansi, our eight-legged friend, was smart. [*Touch your head with your right pointer finger*] Anansi was clever. [*Touch your head with your left pointer finger*] Anansi was even charming. [*Give an exaggerated grin and touch your chin*] But there was one thing Anansi did not have—wisdom. [*Shake pointer finger from side to side*] So Anansi decided that he would collect some wisdom for himself.

He found a large gourd, a vegetable much like a squash, and cut it in half. Scooping out the insides of the gourd, he hollowed it out. [*Motion scooping out a gourd. You can even use a real halved gourd in the story.*] He set it in the sun and let it dry. When it was finished drying, it looked like a big bowl or a giant ice cream scooper. He said, "This is perfect! I shall collect wisdom and store it inside this gourd bowl."

Anansi began his search for wisdom. He sang,

"I need some wisdom.
Where can I get it?
I need some wisdom now."
[*Use a shekere, an African rhythm instrument, which is a gourd covered with shells or beads. Create a rhythm and sing the chorus throughout the story. Ask the audience to join you in singing or chanting.*]

He went to visit his friend, wise old owl. [*Walk to an audience member and bring him/ her to the front of the audience with you. You will direct the drama with your narration, which serves as instruction.*] Owl lived in a tall tree. Anansi stood below the tree and called out, "Owl, oh owl!" [*Ask the audience to call out with you by saying, "Please join in," and repeating the phrase*]

Owl poke his head out of the tree and flapped his wings. [*You can direct Owl by demonstrating the motions*] He answered, "Hoo! Hoo! Who is it?"

"It is I, your friend, Anansi." Anansi held out his gourd and answered, "I am collecting wisdom. Because you are so wise, I thought perhaps you would have wisdom to share with me."

Owl answered, "Of course I do, Anansi." He swooped down from his tree and sprinkled some wisdom from his head into Anansi's gourd. [*Hold out gourd so that Owl can sprinkle wisdom into it*]

Anansi bowed and said, "Thank you, Owl." [*Bow before Owl*]

Owl answered, "My pleasure," and flew back into his tall tree. [*Motion for the audience member to return to his/her chair*]

Anansi looked inside his gourd and saw Owl's wisdom, but it barely filled the bowl. Anansi needed more wisdom, so once again, he began his search for wisdom.

"I need some wisdom.
Where can I get it?
I need some wisdom now."
[*Use a shekere, an African rhythm instrument, which is a gourd covered with shells or beads. Create a rhythm and sing the chorus throughout the story. Ask the audience to join you in singing or chanting.*]

He went to visit his friend, Monkey. [*Walk to an audience member and bring him/her to the front of the audience with you. You will direct the drama with your narration, which serves as instruction.*] Monkey also lived in a tall tree filled with his favorite fruit. Can you guess what his favorite fruit is? [*Give the audience time to answer*] That's right! Bananas! Anansi stood below the tree and called out, "Monkey, oh Monkey!" [*Ask the audience to call out with you by saying, "Please join in," and repeating the phrase*]

Monkey raised one arm over his head, reached over with the other arm and scratched. [*You can direct Monkey by demonstrating the motions*] He answered, "Ooo! Ooo! Eee! Eee! Who is it?"

"It is I, your friend, Anansi." Anansi held out his gourd and answered, "I am collecting wisdom. Because you are wise, I thought perhaps you would have wisdom you to share with me."

Monkey answered, "Of course I do, Anansi," and he climbed down his tree and sprinkled some wisdom from his head into Anansi's gourd. [*Hold out gourd so that Monkey can sprinkle wisdom into it*]

Anansi bowed and said, "Thank you, Monkey." [*Bow before Owl*]

Monkey answered, "Eee. Eee. Eee. No problem." He climbed back up his banana tree. [*Motion for the audience member to return to his/her chair*]

Anansi looked inside his gourd and saw Owl and Monkey's wisdom, but it filled the bowl only halfway. Anansi needed more wisdom, so he began searching. He sang,

"I need some wisdom.
Where can I get it?
I need some wisdom now."
[*Use a shekere, an African rhythm instrument, which is a gourd covered with shells or beads. Create a rhythm and sing the chorus throughout the story. Ask the audience to join you in singing or chanting.*]

He visited his friend Lion, the king of the jungle. [*Walk to an audience member and bring him/her to the front of the audience with you. You will direct the drama with your narration, which serves as instruction.*] Lion lived in a den, a cave located in the side of a steep mountain. Anansi stood in front of the cave and called out, "Lion, oh Lion!" [*Ask the audience to call out with you by saying, "Please join in," and repeating the phrase*]

Lion woke up from his catnap and roared. [*Motion to Lion, signaling him to roar*] "Who is it?"

"It is I, your friend, Anansi." Anansi held out his gourd and answered, "I am collecting wisdom, your majesty. Since you are the king and the wisest animal in the jungle, I thought perhaps you would have great wisdom to share. Do you have any wisdom you can share with me?"

Lion answered, "Of course I do, Anansi." He came out of his cave and sprinkled some wisdom from his head into Anansi's gourd. [*Hold out gourd so that Lion can sprinkle wisdom into it*]

Anansi bowed and said, "Thank you, your highness."

Lion answered, "You are welcome, Anansi."

Anansi looked inside his gourd and saw that it was now . . . [*Pause so that audience can fill in*] full. Now that his gourd was full, Anansi wanted to hide his wisdom so that no one could take it. He spotted a tall tree.

Anansi said, "I will hide my wisdom at the top of that tree." [*Point to the top of a tree*] He tied his gourd to the front of his BIG belly and tried to climb up the tree. [*Mime climbing a tree*] His spidery little legs could not reach the tree. Every time he tried to climb, the gourd would bump the tree and Anansi would fall down. Frustrated, he sat down and began to cry. [*Exaggerate crying. The audience, especially children, find exaggerated crying and sniffling humorous.*]

Just then, his youngest son was walking by. He asked, "Papa, what are you doing?"

Anansi answered, "I am trying to climb up this tree so I can hide my gourd full of wisdom, but I can't seem to make it up the tree." [*Motion to the top of the tree*]

His son answered, "Well, Papa, why don't you tie the gourd to your back instead? That way, you can climb the tree quite easily."

Anansi said, "Alright, son, now go about your business and leave me to mine. I don't need the advice of a child. I can handle this myself."

When his son left, what do you think Anansi did? [*Pause to let the audience fill in*] That's right. Anansi did as his son suggested. He tied the gourd to his back, and to his great delight, he was able to climb up the tree with no problem. [*Mime climbing up the tree*] Once Anansi reached with top of the tree, he looked at his gourd full of wisdom.

"Here I am with all this wisdom, and still, my youngest son is wiser than I! Perhaps I don't need this wisdom after all." With that, Anansi took the gourd and threw the wisdom into the sky. [*Mime throw the wisdom from the gourd*] The wind scooped up that wisdom and spread it around the world so that boys and girls like you could all grab a piece of that wisdom for themselves. [*Ask audience to grab some of that wisdom and tuck it in their heads*] You see, Anansi realized that wisdom should not be kept to oneself. Wisdom must be shared with others. [*Open arms out to audience, signifying sharing wisdom*]

And that, my friends, is how Anansi shared wisdom with the world.

"We have the wisdom
Now we should share it

We have the wisdom now."

[*Use a shekere, an African rhythm instrument, which is a gourd covered with shells or beads. Sing this as you sang chorus throughout the story. Repeat it and ask the audience to join you in singing or chanting.*]

Anansi's Hat Shaking Dance

West Africa

Note from Dianne: *This is a story full of boisterous audience participation. Exaggerate Anansi and make him comical. He is, after all, a trickster. I like telling this story using a real hat (sombrero) and a shekere, maracas, or a clear, plastic bottle filled with beans. With full audience participation, this story can be a good 20 minutes long.*

Audience: Grades 2–6, Ages 7–12

Tell along Techniques:

- Repeating chant/song
- Dramatic pause
- Movement
- Instruments

At the beginning of time, spiders had long hair. But it was a very long time ago . . .

Anansi and his wife were getting ready for a party! [*Do a silly dance*] It was Grandma's birthday. Anansi's wife was cooking up a big, delicious pot of beans for the party. She tasted the beans and said, "These beans are good but they need a little pepper. Let me look in the cupboard for some pepper."

So she opened the cupboard [*Make a creaking sound*] and looked. "Parsley, sage, rosemary, thyme . . . no pepper! I have to run out get some more pepper." She called for her husband, "Anansi!" [*Cup hands around mouth*]

40

He answered, "Yes, dear?!"

Anansi's wife said, "I have to get some more pepper. Will you watch the pot of beans for me?"

Anansi slurped his lips and said, "Yes, dear!" [*Make a slurping sound*]

Anansi's wife knew exactly what he was thinking and said, "Now, Anansi, whatever you do, you musn't touch the beans. Do you understand?"

"Yes, dear."

His wife left and Anansi began decorating for the party. First blew up those big, colorful round things—what do you call them? [*Pause and allow audience to chime in the answer*] Oh yes, balloons! Help me blow up the balloons! [*Have audience help make balloon blowing sounds*]

Then he began hanging up those long colorful paper things—what do you call them? [*Pause and allow audience to chime in the answer*] Oh yes, streamers! Help me snip the streamers. [*Make snipping sounds and motions*]

When he was finished with that, he began setting the table—first the plates, then the glasses, then the silverware, and finally some napkins folded nicely on top of the plates. [*Motion this as you say it*] All that hard work made Anansi very . . . [*Rub your stomach, and the audience will chime in . . .*] hungry! About that time, the aroma of the delicious beans floated in from the kitchen and the beans started to smell REAL good. [*Emphasize REAL with a slurp*]

Anansi went into the kitchen. He looked into the pot of beans. [*Lean in as if you are looking into the pot of beans*] His wife did ask him to "watch" the beans, didn't she? They sure LOOKED good. He took a big whiff of the beans. They sure SMELLED good.

So he stirred the beans.
He smelled the beans.
He tasted the beans.
Mmm. Mmm. Mmm.
They tasted GOOD! [*Give this repeating refrain a hip, catchy chant and invite the audience to join in*]

But one taste wasn't enough. Anansi said, "I'll just have a little . . . [*Pause, and the audience will chime in . . .*] more."

So he stirred the beans.
He smelled the beans.
He tasted the beans.
Mmm. Mmm. Mmm.
They tasted GOOD! [*Repeat the hip, catchy chant with the audience joining in.*]

By now, you can imagine tasting the beans was too much for Anansi. He wanted . . . [*Pause, and the audience will chime in . . .*] more!

So he stirred the beans.
He smelled the beans.
He tasted the beans.
Mmm. Mmm. Mmm.
They tasted good! [*Repeat the hip, catchy chant with the audience joining in*]

Before Anansi knew it, he had eaten more than half of the beans in the pot! "One more small itsy bitsy, teensy weensy, tiny winy little taste couldn't hurt," said Anansi. He was getting ready to put some more beans in his mouth [*Mime this motion*] when he heard the door. [*Make a creaky door sound*]

"Anansi, it's me and Grandma's with me!" his wife called out. [*Cup hands around mouth*]

He heard them walking into the kitchen. [*Pat your hands against your thigh. Motion to the audience to join in.*] He had to think of something and fast! He had to hide the beans! Quickly, he grabbed Grandma's party hat, dumped the beans into the hat, and placed the hat on his head, just as his wife and Grandma were walking into the kitchen. [*Mime these motions as you tell this part of the story: grabbing the hat, dumping the beans, and placing the hat on your head. You may also use a real hat. I like to use a sombrero. It add a humorous element to the story.*]

Now if you know anything about beans coming out of a pot, you know that they are . . . [*Wave your hands in front of your face to signal heat, and the audience will chime in . . .*] hot! They were so hot they were burning the top of Anansi's head! He couldn't stand still and he began shaking and moving around. [*Use a shekere or a plastic bottle filled with beans to create shaking sounds. Dance around as if your head is burning.*]

His wife asked, "Anansi! What are you doing?"

Anansi answered, "Uh, uh, I am doing a new dance for Grandma's party. Yeah, that's it. It's called Anansi's Hat Shaking Dance!" [*Shake the shekere or plastic bottle filled with beans and dance around*]

Grandma said, "Oooh! It looks like fun! I want to dance." And she began to shake and move around, just like Anansi. [*This is a great opportunity for directed role playing. You can pull people from the audience to be Anansi's wife and Grandma. Shake the shekere or plastic bottle filled with beans as Anansi (you) and "Grandma" dance.*]

Anansi's wife looked at Grandma and Anansi shaking and moving and grooving, so she too began to dance! [*Shake the shekere or plastic bottle filled with beans as Anansi (you), "Grandma," and "Anansi's wife" dance*]

But all that movin' and shakin' was a-movin' and a-shakin' those beans! The heat on top of Anansi's head was too much! The beans began to drip down the side of his face—down his cheeks, down his neck, and even in his ears! [*Mime these motions and allow the audience to chime in . . .*] Eeeeww! Finally, he couldn't take it anymore and he jerked off the hat. [*Pull the real or imaginary hat off*]

Anansi's wife cried out, "Anansi, just what did you think you were doing?!" She put her hands on her hips, just like your mama does when she's mad. [*Place hands on hips*]

Anansi smiled sheepishly at his wife and said, "I couldn't help it!"

I stirred the beans.
I smelled the beans.
I tasted the beans.
Mmm. Mmm. Mmm.
They tasted good! [*Repeat the hip, catchy chant with the audience joining in*]

Anansi's wife looked into the pot and saw how much of the beans were missing. [*Mime looking into the pot*] "Anansi!" she cried out.

But Grandma started laughing hysterically. [*Laugh big deep belly laughs and mime pointing*] She pointed to Anansi's head and said, "Boy, you are as bald as a bowling ball!" [*Allow a few moments for the audience to laugh*]

Anansi's wife started laughing too, and Grandma said she never laughed so hard in all her life. It was one of the funniest, best birthday gifts she had ever received. And because Grandma was happy, everyone was happy.

There was still a little bit of beans left in the pot, so they shared. One more time . . .

They stirred the beans.
They smelled the beans.
They tasted the beans.
Mmm. Mmm. Mmm.
They tasted . . . [*Pause and allow audience to chime in loud . . .*] GOOD!

They had a great time at Grandma's birthday party and even danced a brand new dance—Anansi's Hat Shaking Dance. [*Shake the shekere or plastic bottle filled with beans and dance around*]

To this day, if you look at a spider, you will see that he is still bald, but he sure knows how to dance!

The Bag of Truth

Spain

Note from Dianne: I love this story because it casts the poor son of a farmer as the hero who gets the girl in the end. It's a funny tale, and the children will enjoy putting the "truth into the bag." Differentiate the voices of Pedro and the king by giving the king a deep, rich voice.

Audience: Grades 3–6, Ages 8–12

Tell along Techniques:

- Repeating chant/song

- Dramatic pause

- Repeating movement

Once, on the far side of yesterday, a poor son of a farmer had saved the princess's life by giving her magic pears that made her well when she was sick. This young man was named Pedro, and the king said Pedro could have anything in the world he wanted.

Pedro said, "Though I am the poor son of the farmer, I wish to marry the princess."

Although the king was grateful to Pedro for his deed, the king did not want the poor son of a farmer to marry his daughter. The king called for his hare. (And I don't mean the kind on your head. [*Point to your head*] I mean the kind that hops! [*Hop up and down*]) A hare is a . . . [*Allow audience to chime in*] rabbit! A servant handed the king a

44

From *Tell Along Tales!: Playing with Participation Stories* by Dianne de Las Casas. Santa Barbara, CA: Libraries Unlimited. Copyright © 2011.

hare branded with the king's mark. The king said, "If, in a year, you can call this hare to you, you may marry the princess."

Pedro said, "Done deal! I will return here in a year and call the hare to me."

So Pedro set off for the woods. He made friends with all the animals when he blew on his . . . [*Pause and invite audience to say "magic silver whistle" with you*] magic silver whistle and the animals came to him. At the end of the year, he blew on his . . . [*Pause to allow audience to chime in*] magic silver whistle and called the hare with the king's mark. He walked to the castle with the hare in his arms.

The king of Spain looked out of the window and saw Pedro walking with the hare in his arms. He said, "Oh no! That poor son of a farmer is back to marry my daughter! I need to get that hare away from him." He sent a servant with a bag of gold and said, "Buy that hare from that boy."

The servant bought the hare from Pedro, and Pedro took the gold. As soon as the servant reached the castle, Pedro blew on his . . . [*Pause to allow audience to chime in*] magic silver whistle and called the hare with the king's mark. He continued walking to the castle with the hare in his arms.

The king of Spain said, "Oh no! That poor son of a farmer is back to marry my daughter! I need to get that hare away from him." He sent the princess and said, "Convince Pedro to give you that hare."

The princess batted her eyelashes at Pedro, [*Make a pretty princess face*] and Pedro gave her the hare. As soon as the princess reached the castle, Pedro blew on his . . . [*Pause to allow audience to chime in*] magic silver whistle and called the hare with the king's mark. He continued walking to the castle with the hare in his arms.

The king of Spain said, "I will have to get that hare myself!"

So the king went to Pedro and said, "I will give you ten bags of gold for that hare."

Pedro answered, "You can have the hare for nothing if you will kiss him."

The king was very angry, but he had to have that hare because his didn't want his daughter to marry the poor son of a farmer! So he made sure no one looking and kissed the hare behind a tree. [*Put your hand in front of your face and make big smacking kiss sounds*] Pedro gave the king the hare and followed the king to the castle.

Pedro said to everyone, "It has been a year and I am here to marry the king's beautiful daughter."

The King's Court was surprised. A princess could not marry a poor son of a farmer! The king knew he could not break his promise, so he said, "There is one more thing you must do before you marry the princess. You must fill this big bag with Truth."

Pedro said, "I will gladly fill a bag with Truth right here in the castle."

Pedro opened the big bag and said to the king, "Is it true that I brought a basket of the most beautiful pears in Spain to the princess?"

"Yes," said the king. "That is the truth."

Pedro said [*The first time, invite the audience to say the following lines and do the motions*]

"Wickety, wack, wickety wack. [*Clap with each word*]

Truth, truth, jump into my sack." [*Snap with the word "truth" and cradle one arm and point into the "hole" with your other hand when you say "into my sack"*]

Pedro said to the king, "Is it true that the pears made the princess well?"

"Yes," said the king. "That is the truth."

Pedro said, [*Audience participates with storyteller*] "Wickety, wack, wickety wack. [*Clap with each word*]

Truth, truth, jump into my sack." [*Snap with the word "truth" and cradle one arm and point into the "hole" with your other hand when you say "into my sack"*]

Pedro said to the king, "Is it true that the king promised me I could marry the princess if, in a year, I would call the hare with the king's mark?"

"Yes," said the king. "That is the truth."

Pedro said, [*Audience participates with storyteller*] "Wickety, wack, wickety wack. [*Clap with each word*]

Truth, truth, jump into my sack." [*Snap with the word "truth" and cradle one arm and point into the "hole" with your other hand when you say "into my sack"*]

Pedro said to the king, "Is it true that the king wanted to get out of his promise and that he kissed . . ."

"Stop! Stop!" cried the king. "The bag is now filled with truth. You may marry the princess."

So Pedro, the poor son of a farmer, and the beautiful princess were married, and they lived happily all the rest of their days. The clock has run. My tale is done.

The Bobtail Monkey

Japan

Note from Dianne: *This story is a story about consequences. The monkey in this tale is foolish, impatient, and a braggart. But his antics are funny, and children will laugh at his bobtail. In the beginning of the story, tell the audience, "Every time you hear the word 'monkey,' raise one arm and say 'ooh, ooh, ooh.' Then raise the other arm and say, 'Eeh, Eeh, Eeh.'"*

This is a rehearsed call and response, and it lends a hilarious element to the story as the whole audience becomes a monkey.

Audience: Grades 2–6, Ages 7–12

Tell along Techniques:

- Repeating chant/song
- Call and response
- Movement

Once there was a monkey. [*Audience and storyteller to say together, "Ooh, ooh, ooh" and "Eeh, Eeh, Eeh" with arm motions*] He was always playing tricks and doing foolish things. Everyone warned him to be more careful, but he never listened.

One day, he was swinging through the trees when he fell right into the middle of a big thorn bush. A long, sharp thorn went right through the tip of his tail.

A barber happened by with a razor in his hand. When he saw the monkey, [*Audience and storyteller to say together, "Ooh, ooh, ooh" and "Eeh, Eeh, Eeh" with arm motions*] he offered to cut out the thorn. But the little animal was sooo impatient that he jumped up

47

as the razor came down, and the barber accidentally cut off his tail, leaving him with a bobtail.

Monkey [*Audience and storyteller to say together, "Ooh, ooh, ooh" and "Eeh, Eeh, Eeh" with arm motions*] jumped and rubbed his rump. [*Mime rubbing your rump. The kids will laugh.*] He cried out, [*Invite the audience to say the story chorus with you*]

"Look, just look at what you have done! I had a tail and now I have none!"
The barber felt bad so he gave our little friend his razor.

Monkey [*Audience and storyteller to say together, "Ooh, ooh, ooh" and "Eeh, Eeh, Eeh" with arm motions*] moved on and met an old woman gathering wood. He said, "You can use my razor to cut your wood." The old woman used the razor, but razors are not meant for cutting wood, and soon, his razor was ragged, jagged, and totally useless. Our friend cried out, [*Audience to participate with storyteller*]

"Look, just look at what you have done!
I had a . . . [*Pause to allow audience to chime in*] razor and now I have none!"
The old woman felt bad so she gave our little friend her wood.

Monkey [*Audience and storyteller to say together, "Ooh, ooh, ooh" and "Eeh, Eeh, Eeh" with arm motions*] moved on and met another old woman baking cookies. He said, "You can use my wood to bake your cookies." The old woman used the firewood, but eventually, the fire ate it up and turned it to ash. Our friend cried out, [*Audience to participate with storyteller*]

"Look, just look at what you have done!
I had some [*Pause to allow audience to chime in*] wood, now I have none!"
The old woman felt bad, so she gave our little friend her cookies.

Monkey [*Audience and storyteller to say together, "Ooh, ooh, ooh" and "Eeh, Eeh, Eeh" with arm motions*] moved on and met an old man with a brass gong. He said to the old man, "You can have my cookies if you give me your gong." So the old man agreed.

Monkey [*Audience and storyteller to say together, "Ooh, ooh, ooh" and "Eeh, Eeh, Eeh" with arm motions*] ran with his gong and climbed the highest tree. He hung the gong and banged a song. [*Teach to audience and have them sing with you*]

"I'm a handsome little fellow
The smartest in the land
With my fine brass gong
I'm the leader of the band."

BING! BONG! BONG!
BING! BONG! BONG!

He danced and danced on top of the branch, bragging about his gong when suddenly . . . Well, what do you think happened? [*Pause to allow audience to answer*] That's right! He fell and fell from the branch landing in a . . . big thorn bush!

From that time on, everyone called him Bobtail Bong-Bong because he was such a foolish little . . . MONKEY! [*Audience and storyteller to say together, "Ooh, ooh, ooh" and "Eeh, Eeh, Eeh" with arm motions*]

The Bremen Town Musicians

Germany

Note from Dianne: This is a great story to use with different instruments. If you cannot play any instruments, use various rhythm instruments (maracas, shekere, guiro tone block, sand blocks, and so on). It is also a great story to use for directed role playing. Audience members can volunteer to enact the parts of the donkey, the dog, the cat, and the rooster.

Audience: Grades 1–6, Ages 6–12

Tell along Techniques:

- Repeating chant/song
- Dramatic pause
- Directed role playing
- Movement
- Instruments

In ages past, when animals spoke their minds, there was a farmer who had a faithful donkey. For years, the beast of burden carried heavy sacks back and forth to the mill and the market. But alas, he was growing old and was no longer able to carry his weight around the farm. At night, Donkey would comfort himself with his music. [*Play an instrument and create a tune or a rhythm*] Though Donkey had served the farmer well,

50

the farmer needed someone more useful, and he asked Donkey to leave. [*If you want to try directed role playing, you can request a volunteer from the audience to play the donkey. Be sure to articulate quiet but clear instructions to the participant.*]

"What will I do?" cried Donkey? "I can no longer carry heavy loads. I am old and useless. No one wants me around." He began playing his music to comfort himself. [*Play an instrument and create a sad tune or a rhythm*] That is when inspiration hit!

"I know! I will become a jazz musician in Bremen Town. I will play my music and make people happy." [*You can invite participation here. Pause after the "and" and ask the audience to repeat "make people happy" a couple of times. Each time this refrain appears in the story, the audience will join in.*] Excited, he began following his dream down the road. His new purpose made him fleet of foot, and he trolloped happily down the road. [*Play instrument in an excited mood or instruct volunteer to do so*]

It wasn't long before he heard some sad music. [*Play an instrument and create a sad tune or a rhythm*] He saw a droopy-eared dog sadly drumming by the side of the road. Donkey asked, "Dog, why are you so sad?" [*You can request a volunteer from the audience to play the dog. Articulate quiet but clear instructions to the participant.*]

Dog whined, "I am old and useless. No one wants me around."

Donkey replied, "Why don't you come with me to Bremen Town and become a musician? We'll have a jazz band! We'll play our music and . . . make people happy." [*Pause after the "and," and the audience will join in saying, "make people happy"*]

Dog wagged his tail excitedly and yelped, "Yes, I will!" [*Instruct volunteer to "wag" his tail. The audience will laugh.*]

So Donkey and Dog began following their dream down the road. [*Have volunteers play instruments in an excited mood. Add some dance moves.*]

It wasn't long before they heard some sad music. [*Play an instrument and create a sad tune or a rhythm*] They saw a cat, who had lost her cool, sadly playing an instrument. Donkey asked, "Cat, why are you so sad?" [*You can request a volunteer from the audience to play the cat. Articulate quiet but clear instructions to the participant.*]

Cat sniffed, "I am old and useless. No one wants me around."

Donkey replied, "Why don't you come with us to Bremen Town and become a musician? We'll have a jazz band! We'll play our music and . . . make people happy." [*Pause after the "and," and the audience will join in saying, "make people happy"*]

Cat purred and said, "Yes, I will!" [*Have the "cat" purr*]

So Donkey, Dog, and Cat began following their dream down the road. [*Have volunteers play instruments in an excited mood with fun dance moves*]

It wasn't long before they heard more sad music. [*Play an instrument and create a sad tune or a rhythm*] They saw a rooster, whose feathers were ruffled, sadly playing his music. Donkey asked, "Rooster, why are you so sad?" [*You can request a volunteer from the audience to play the rooster. Articulate quiet but clear instructions to the participant.*]

Rooster cried, "I am old and useless. No one wants me around."

Donkey replied, "Why don't you come with us to Bremen Town and become a musician? We'll have a jazz band! We'll play our music and . . . make people happy." [*Pause after the "and," and the audience will join in saying, "make people happy"*]

Rooster crowed and said, "Yes, I will!"

So Donkey, Dog, Cat, and Rooster began following their dream down the road. [*Have volunteers play instruments in an excited mood with fun dance moves*]

The sun began to sink, and it was growing dark. They found a big oak tree in the forest and settled around it, finding comfortable spots to sleep. Rooster perched himself on a high branch and saw a cottage in the distance with a light on.

Rooster called out to his friends, "I see a cottage not far away. Perhaps we can sleep there!" The other animals agreed, and they set off for the cottage. [*Everyone plays their instruments as they "march" to the cottage*] When they arrived, Donkey stood on his hind legs and peeked in the window. Inside the cottage were robbers counting their gold!

Donkey said, "There are robbers! We must get rid of them. I think I have a plan!" Donkey and the animals huddled together. [*Gather all the volunteers in a huddle*] After a little while, Donkey, Dog, Cat and Rooster set up below the window and began playing the most awful music you have ever heard. [*Have volunteers made a racket*] The sounds shattered the window. [*Clang some cymbals*]

The robbers heard the thundering noise and were scared out of their wits, thinking a monster was coming in for them. They ran out of the cottage in the forest.

When the robbers were gone, Donkey and his friends went inside the cottage. They had a nice, warm meal and settled down for the night. Donkey stretched out on some straw, Dog lay near the door, Cat curled up by the fireplace, and Rooster perched on a beam in the ceiling. [*Have all the volunteers lie down to "sleep"*]

Meanwhile, the robbers became bold. One of the robbers returned to the cottage and crept near the fireplace to light a match. As soon as he bent over, Cat woke up [*Have "cat" hiss*] and scratched him all over. Dog woke up [*Have dog bark*] and bit the robber in the leg. Rooster woke up [*Have rooster crow*] and landed on top of the robber's head. Donkey woke up [*Have donkey hee haw*] and kicked the robber out of the cottage. The robber ran back into the forest screaming about a monster. The rest of the robbers decided that the cottage was haunted, and they never returned.

Donkey, Dog, Cat and Rooster made the cottage their home. They followed their dream down the road to Bremen Town and became the hippest jazz musicians around. They played their music and . . . made people happy. [*Pause after the "and," and the audience will join in saying, "make people happy"*]

Even now, you can travel to the town of Bremen and see a large statue honoring the four friends who dared to follow a dream. [*Have volunteers play their instruments and dance one more time*]

[*At the end, have everyone hold hands. You say, "1-2-3, Take a bow with me." The volunteers will bow as the audience applauds.*]

Elephant and Snake

United States

Note from Dianne: *This is a story from Louisiana. It's surprising because it rarely snows in the South and there are no elephants in the bayou (that I know of). But it is a fun story, and I have added some funky hip-hop rhythms to the refrains. Play with the sounds and change them if you want. The goal is to have a consistent chorus that the audience will enjoy repeating with you as you tell the story. Lapin is pronounced "lah-PAN" with a very soft "N" at the end. It means "rabbit" in French.*

Audience: Grades K–4, Ages 5–10

Tell along Techniques:

- Repeating chant/song
- Repeating refrains
- Movement

Brrrrrr. It was a cold day in Louisiana. It was so cold that snow fell and covered everything. Elephant was walking through the woods.

BOOM. BOOM. BOOM.
BOOM. BOOM. BOOM. [*Create a fun, funky rhythm and even a dance move*]
As he was walking, he came upon a log. The log began to talk!

54

"Please help me! I am sssssssooooo cold!" [*Every time Snake speaks, exaggerate the "S" in his words*] Elephant had never seen a talking log before, so he bent down to take a closer look. A snake hissed!

Sssssssssssssssssssssssssssssssssssssssssssssssssssssssssss

Elephant jumped back. [*Jump back as you say this*] "Oy, it's not a talking log. It's a snake, stuck under a log!"

Snake said, "Yesssssss. I am sssstuck. Pleasssssse help me out from under this log."

Elephant asked, "Why are you stuck, Snake?"

Snake answered, "I was cold ssssso I thought that I could get warm under the log. I ssssslipped under the log, and now I am sssssssstuck! Please help me out."

Elephant said, "Okay," and lifted the log with his trunk. Snake slithered next to Elephant. [*Make a slithering motion with your hand and arm*]

Snake said, "I am sssstill cold. Could I slide up your leg to keep warm?"

Elephant agreed and . . .

Snake slip slippety slid up Elephant's leg.

Sssssssss. Sssssssssss. Sssssssss. [*Chant this in a fun, funky rhythm while making slithering motions with your hand and arm*]

"Snake said, "I am sssstill cold. Could I slide up your waisssst to keep warm?"

Elephant agreed and . . .

Snake slip slippety slid up Elephant's waist.

Sssssssss. Sssssssssss. Sssssssss. [*Chant this in a fun, funky rhythm while making slithering motions with your hand and arm*]

"Snake said, "I am sssstill cold. Could I slide up your arm to keep warm?"

Elephant agreed and . . .

Snake slip slippety slid up Elephant's arm.

Sssssssss. Sssssssssss. Sssssssss. [*Chant this in a fun, funky rhythm while making slithering motions with your hand and arm*]

Then Snake looked at Elephant and said, "Now I am going to bite you!"

Elephant cried out, "But I just helped you. You can't bite me!"

Snake replied, "That's what I do. I am a sssssnake and sssssnakes bite."

Elephant said, "Wait! Let's talk to Lapin, our friend rabbit. If he thinks it is fair for you to bite me, then I will let you bite me."

Snake agreed, and they set off to find Lapin.

BOOM. BOOM. BOOM.
Sssssssss. Sssssssssss. Sssssssss.
BOOM. BOOM. BOOM.
Sssssssss. Sssssssssss. Sssssssss. [*Continue the fun, funky rhythm and dance moves*]

When they found Lapin, Elephant explained the situation. Then he said, "So Lapin, if you agree that it is fair for Snake to bite me, then I will let him bite me."

Lapin thought for a moment. "Well, the only way I can make a decision is to see the log for myself. Show me where it is."

So Elephant, Snake, and Lapin traveled to the log.

BOOM BOOM BOOM
Sssssssss. Ssssssssss. Sssssssss.
Hippety Hop. Hop. Hop
BOOM BOOM BOOM
Sssssssss. Ssssssssss. Sssssssss.
Hippety Hop. Hop. Hop [*Continue the fun, funky rhythm and dance moves*]

When they reached the log, Lapin said, "Snake, I need you to show me exactly how you were stuck."

"Certainly," said Snake, as he slip slippety slid under the log. [*Make slithering motions with your hand and arm*]

Lapin asked, "Snake, are you good and stuck?"

Snake answered, "Yessssss."

Lapin laughed, "Good! Now stay stuck!"

Then Elephant and Lapin set off for a steaming hot cup of carrot tea.

BOOM BOOM BOOM
Hippety Hop. Hop. Hop
BOOM BOOM BOOM
Hippety Hop. Hop. Hop [*Continue the fun, funky rhythm and dance moves*]

Snake learned his lesssssson and never threatened to bite Elephant again. The End.

Fortunately, Unfortunately

Original

Note from Dianne: *"Fortunately, Unfortunately" is actually an improvisation word play game where players create the story as they go, switching between "fortunately" and "unfortunately." There is a book by Remy Charlip titled* Fortunately *published in 1993 that chronicles the adventures of a boy named Ned who tries to get to a party. It follows the same pattern as the "Good News, Bad News" or "That's Good! That's Bad" types of stories. I have used the nursery rhyme "Mary Had a Little Lamb" as the basis for this story. The audience will need to be directed ahead of time to say "fortunately" and "unfortunately." It's not a long story and works well as a fun filler.*

Audience: Grades 3–6, Ages 8–12

Tell along Techniques:

- Repeating chant/song
- Dramatic pause
- Rehearsed response

Mary had a little lamb and decided to bring her pet lamb to school. It was so cute! Its fleece was as white as snow. But . . .

[*The audience chimes in . . .*] Unfortunately . . .

The lamb stepped in a big pile of dog doo doo. [*Allow audience to laugh*] The lamb was no longer white, and boy, did she stink! But . . .

[*The audience chimes in . . .*] Fortunately . . .

The neighbor had a hose. Mary turned on the hose and began spraying her lamb down. The lamb's fleece was becoming white again! But . . .

[*The audience chimes in . . .*] Unfortunately . . .

Mary accidentally sprayed a lady walking by. The lady got soaking wet and happened to be Mary's mom . . . [*Allow audience to gasp*] Uh oh! But . . .

[*The audience chimes in . . .*] Fortunately . . .

It started to pour. Everyone was getting soaked anyway. Mary's mom offered Mary a ride to school in her brand new candy apple red Corvette! But . . .

[*The audience chimes in . . .*] Unfortunately . . .

Mary's lamb started running away, and Mary had to chase the lamb down the street. Mary was late to school, she was soaking wet, and her lamb was on the lam! But . . .

[*The audience chimes in . . .*] Fortunately . . .

Mary's friend, Jack came around the corner. Jack was nimble. Jack was quick. Jack jumped on his horse on a stick and lassoed Mary's lamb. But . . .

[*The audience chimes in . . .*] Unfortunately . . .

The lasso broke, and the lamb was on the loose! Mary ran, and Jack giddy-upped down the road chasing the runaway rogue. The lamb was getting away! But . . .

[*The audience chimes in . . .*] Fortunately . . .

The lamb ran all the way to Mary's school. Mary asked Little Bo Peep to watch after her sheep. Little Boy Blue played his horn, and the baby sheep fell . . . asleep. Mary finally got to school and had a great story to tell! But . . .

[*The audience chimes in . . .*] Unfortunately . . .

Her school principal didn't want to hear it!

The Golden Goose

Germany

Note from Dianne: *This is a fun story with a lot of audience participation. If you are just starting out with audience participation, I recommend telling it without volunteers to act out the story on stage with you. If you are more experienced, this is a perfect story to do with directed role playing. The cumulative refrain in this story makes it easy to learn.*

Audience: Grades 2–6, Ages 7–12

Tell along Techniques:

- Repeating chant/song
- Dramatic pause
- Directed role playing
- Repeating motions

There was once a man who had three sons. The youngest was named Simple Simon. One day, the oldest son had to go into the forest to chop wood. His mother gave him a tasty pancake and a jug of juice. When he reached the forest, he met an old dwarf.

The dwarf asked, "Will you please share your food and drink with me?"

The oldest son refused. Then he began chopping the wood.

Chippety, chop, chop, chop, chop, chop
Chippety, chop, chop, chop, chop, chop [*Mime chopping and have audience join in the story chorus. Give it a fun, hip rhythm.*]

59

Suddenly, the axe went flying, and the oldest son hurt himself. He returned home with no wood.

The next day, the second-oldest son had to go into the forest to chop wood. His mother gave him a tasty pancake and a jug of juice. When he reached the forest, he met an old dwarf.

The dwarf asked, "Will you please share your food and drink with me?"

The oldest son refused. Then he began chopping the wood.

Chippety, chop, chop, chop, chop, chop
Chippety, chop, chop, chop, chop, chop [*Mime chopping, and the audience will join in the story chorus. Repeat the fun, hip rhythm.*]

Suddenly, the axe went flying, and the second-oldest son hurt himself. He returned home with no wood.

The very next day, Simple Simon asked to chop wood in the forest. His father agreed. His mother gave him a stale piece of bread and a jug of sour juice. When he reached the forest, Simple Simon met an old dwarf.

The dwarf asked, "Will you please share your food and drink with me?" [*Use an "old" voice for the voice of the dwarf*]

Simple Simon said, "Of course." So they began to eat. The stale bread turned into a delicious cake, and the sour juice turned into sweet nectar. The dwarf was so pleased he said to Simple Simon, "Since you have been so kind, I have a gift for you. Chop this tree, and inside you will find your treasure."

Then Simple Simon began chopping the wood.

Chippety, chop, chop, chop, chop, chop
Chippety, chop, chop, chop, chop, chop [*Mime chopping, and the audience will join in the story chorus. Repeat the fun, hip rhythm.*]

Inside the tree, he found a golden goose! He began traveling towards town when a milkmaid spotted him. She said, "A golden goose. Surely one feather will . . . make me rich!" [*Invite the audience to say, "make me rich," and they will continue to repeat it if you pause after "Surely one feather will . . ."*] She grabbed Simple Simon and became stuck! The milkmaid cried,

Let me loose! Let me loose!
I'm stuck to the man with the golden goose. [*Invite the audience to join in this cumulative chorus. As the refrain repeats and builds on, the audience will catch on. If you are experienced at story time, this is fun to bring volunteers from the audience for directed role playing.*]

Simon and the milkmaid continued traveling to town. Once in town, the shoemaker looked out of his window to see the spectacle. He said, "A golden goose. Surely one feather will . . . make me rich!" [*Pause after "Surely one feather will . . ." and allow audience to chime in, "make me rich!"*] He grabbed the milkmaid and became stuck! The shoemaker cried,

> Let me loose! Let me loose!
> I'm stuck to the milkmaid who's stuck to the man with the golden goose. [*The audience will at least say, "Let me loose! Let me loose!" if you pause after "The shoemaker cried . . ." They will also chime in with "golden goose" automatically as the story progresses.*]

Simon, the shoemaker, and the milkmaid continued traveling through town. The baker looked out of his window to see the spectacle. He said, "A golden goose. Surely one feather will . . . make me rich!" [*Pause after "Surely one feather will . . ." and allow audience to chime in "make me rich!"*] He grabbed the shoemaker and became stuck! The baker cried,

> Let me loose! Let me loose!
> I'm stuck to the shoemaker who's stuck to the
> milkmaid who's stuck to the
> man with the golden goose. [*Allow audience to join in*]

Simon, the baker, the shoemaker, and the milkmaid continued traveling through town. The tailor looked out of his window to see the spectacle. He said, "A golden goose. Surely one feather will . . . make me rich!" [*Pause after "Surely one feather will . . ." and allow audience to chime in "make me rich!"*] He grabbed the baker and became stuck! The tailor cried,

> Let me loose! Let me loose!
> I'm stuck to the baker who's stuck to the
> shoemaker who's stuck to the
> milkmaid who's stuck to the
> man with the golden goose. [*Allow audience to join in*]

Simon, the tailor, the baker, the shoemaker, and the milkmaid continued traveling through town. The chef looked out of his window to see the spectacle. He said, "A golden goose. Surely one feather will . . . make me rich!" [*Pause after "Surely one feather will . . ." and allow audience to chime in "make me rich!"*] He grabbed the tailor and became stuck! The chef cried,

Let me loose! Let me loose!
I'm stuck to the tailor who's stuck to the
baker who's stuck to the
shoemaker who's stuck to the
milkmaid who's stuck to the
man with the golden goose. [*It becomes really comical if you speed up the cumulative refrain and pause only to allow the audience to chime in "golden goose!"*]

Simon, the chef, the tailor, the baker, the shoemaker, and the milkmaid continued traveling. They happened to be traveling in front of a castle. A very sad princess, who had not laughed in years, looked out of her window to see the spectacle. The chef continued to cry,

Let me loose! Let me loose!
I'm stuck to the tailor who's stuck to the
baker who's stuck to the
shoemaker who's stuck to the
milkmaid who's stuck to the
man with the golden goose. [*Continue the sped-up cumulative refrain and pause only to allow the audience to chime in "golden goose!"*]

The princess began to laugh hysterically. [*Laugh in an exaggerated manner*] The king was pleased to see his daughter laughing again. He asked to see the man with the golden goose. He said to Simple Simon, "You may marry my daughter if you can empty all of the barrels in my apple cider cellar by midnight."

So Simple Simon went to the old dwarf in the forest. He said, "Since you are always thirsty, I know where you can quench your thirst." Simon took the dwarf to the apple cider cellar, and the dwarf emptied every last barrel. [*Make big slurping sounds and mime as if you are drinking all the cider from barrels*]

The next day, the king said, "You may marry my daughter if you can find a man who can eat a mountain of bread by midnight."

So Simple Simon went to the old dwarf in the forest. He said, "Since you are always hungry, I know where you can fill your belly." Simon took the dwarf to the mountain of bread and the dwarf ate every last crumb. [*Make loud eating and burping noises and mime as if you are devouring all the bread*]

Then the king said, "You may marry my daughter if you can give me a ship that can sail on land and on water."

So Simple Simon went to the old dwarf in the forest. He said, "Will you please give me a ship that can sail on land and on water?" Since Simple Simon was so kind to the dwarf, the dwarf gave him the ship. Then Simple Simon gave the ship to the king. The king had no choice but to give his daughter's hand in marriage to . . . Simple Simon. [*Pause and allow the audience to answer, "Simple Simon!"*]

Simple Simon and the princess were married. [*Make exaggerated kissing sounds. If you are telling to elementary-age children, they will automatically respond, "Ewwww!"*] Simon inherited the kingdom and ruled with his beautiful wife and his golden goose. And they lived . . . [*Pause and allow audience to chime in "happily ever after"*] The End.

The Gourd of Honey

Haiti

Note from Dianne: *This is a classic trickster tale that originated in Africa. There are many variants of this story. In the Louisiana variant, Lapin (Rabbit) is the trickster and takes advantage of Bouqui (Fox). In this Haitian version, Malice is the trickster who takes advantage of Bouqui. This is a fun story because the audience will realize what Malice is doing before Bouqui does. In some variants, Malice is punished, but I let him get away with eating all the honey because he was so clever in how he tricked Bouqui.*

Audience: Grades 4–6, Ages 9–12

Tell along Techniques:

- Audience query
- Repeating chant/song
- Dramatic pause

Bouqui had a big gourd of honey that he was saving for a special occasion, and Malice was jealous that Bouqui had all that honey and would not share. One day, Bouqui and Malice were working in the field under the hot sun. Malice was getting tired and started thinking about having a sweet honey refreshment. There was a problem. Malice did not have any honey. Who had the honey? [*Allow the audience to answer "Bouqui"*]

So Malice came up with a plan. He said,

[*Invite the audience to say the following story chorus with you*]

64

From *Tell Along Tales!: Playing with Participation Stories* by Dianne de Las Casas. Santa Barbara, CA: Libraries Unlimited. Copyright © 2011.

"Put down my hoe, 1, 2, 3
I have to go, someone's calling for me!"
Bouqui said, "I heard nothing but a sheep." [*Say "Baa, baa, baa" and have audience join in*]

But Malice dashed off and left. He went to Bouqui's house because Bouqui had the . . . [*Allow audience to chime in*] honey! Malice slippity slurped up that honey. [*Make fun slurping sounds*]

When he returned to the field, Bouqui asked, "Where did you go?"

Malice answered, "I am a godfather, and I had to baptize a baby."

Bouqui asked, "What did you name the baby?"

Malice replied, "Début." [*Say to the audience, "Début in Creole French means 'beginning'"*]

Bouqui said, "That is an unusual name but so be it." He continued working in the field.

A little while later, Malice started thinking about having some sweet honey again. But there was a problem. Malice did not have any honey. Who had the honey? [*Allow the audience to answer "Bouqui"*]

So Malice said,
[*Audience to participate with storyteller*]

"Put down my hoe, 1, 2, 3
I have to go, someone's calling for me!"
Bouqui said, "I heard nothing but a cow." [*Say "Moo, moo, moo" and have audience join in*]

But Malice dashed off and left. He went to Bouqui's house because Bouqui had the . . . [*Allow audience to chime in*] honey! Malice slippity slurped up that honey. [*Make fun slurping sounds*]

When he returned to the field, Bouqui asked, "Where did you go?"

Malice answered, "I am a godfather, and I had to baptize another baby."

Bouqui asked, "What did you name the baby?"

Malice replied, "Dèmi." [*Say to the audience, "Dèmi in Creole French means 'halfway'"*]

Bouqui said, "That is an unusual name, but so be it." He continued working in the field.

A little while later, Malice started thinking about having some sweet honey again. But there was a problem. Malice did not have any honey. Who had the honey? [*Allow the audience to answer "Bouqui"*]

So Malice said,
[*Audience to participate with storyteller*]

"Put down my hoe, 1, 2, 3
I have to go, someone's calling for me!"
Bouqui said, "I heard nothing but a dog." [*Say "Arf, arf, arf" and have audience join in*]

But Malice dashed off and left. He went to Bouqui's house because Bouqui had the . . . [*Allow audience to chime in*] honey! Malice slippity slurped up that honey. [*Make fun slurping sounds*]

When he returned to the field, Bouqui asked, "Where did you go?"

Malice answered, "I am a godfather, and I had to baptize the last baby."

Bouqui asked, "What did you name the baby?"

Malice replied, "Sèche." [*Say to the audience, "Sèche in Creole French means 'dry'"*]

Bouqui said, "That is an unusual name but so be it." But Bouqui was getting tired now. He said, "Let's go to my house and celebrate all those babies by having some of my sweet, delicious . . . [*Allow audience to chime in*] honey!

Uh oh! Malice didn't know what to do. He followed Bouqui to his house. Bouqui pulled out the gourd but it was . . . [*Allow audience to chime in*] empty! Malice said, "Well, since there is no honey, I'd better be going now!" He dashed off and left.

Bouqui was quite puzzled. How did his honey disappear? Then he started thinking . . . "Début, Dèmi and Sèche! Beginning, Halfway and Dry! Malice was beginning my honey, then he was halfway through my honey, and now my honey is dry! Why, that dirty, rotten, no-good sad excuse for a friend!" It was quite some time before Bouqui would speak to Malice again.

Meanwhile, Malice was quite full of sweet, delicious . . . [*Allow audience to chime in*] honey! That night, he slept just like a . . . baby!

It Could Always Be Worse!

Eastern Europe (Yiddish)

Note from Dianne: This story is liberally adapted from a Yiddish tale. It is a fun story to use with call-and-response audience participation. It will require some advance coaching in the beginning, but the audience will soon catch on. If you are brave, you can also use the directed role-playing technique, in which audience members come to the stage and play the roles of the animals in the story. This story actually breaks the rule of "3 to 5," but it is the chaos of the animals in this story that becomes the turning point of the tale. A special thank-you goes to Jay Menes, a phenomenal storyteller and good friend from Manila. Jay came up with the chorus for this story during a workshop I taught in the Philippines.

Audience: Grades 1–6, Ages 6–12

Tell along Techniques:

- Call and response
- Directed role playing
- Repeating chant/song
- Dramatic pause
- Movement

A great while ago, in a small village was a man who lived in a small house with his wife and seven children. It was crowded and noisy. Wanting peace, the man went to seek the wise counsel of the Rabbi.

The man said, "Rabbi, my life is so miserable. I am in a small house with my wife and our seven children. It is always crowded and noisy. What should I do?" The Rabbi said,

"It could always be worse!"

Then the Rabbi said, "Get a dog." So the man got a dog. [*Use a volunteer from the audience to play the dog*] The wife whined, the children cried, and the dog barked [*Dog barks*].

Who let the dogs out?! [*Storyteller*]
"Woof, woof, woof, woof" [*Audience*]
Who let the dogs out?! [*Storyteller*]
"Woof, woof, woof, woof" [*Audience*]

The man went back to the Rabbi and said, "Rabbi, my life is so miserable. I am in a small house with my wife, our seven children, and a barking dog. It is always crowded and noisy. What should I do?" The Rabbi said, [*Pause and allow the audience to chime in*]

"It could always be worse!"

Then the Rabbi said, "Get a cat." So the man got a cat. [*Use a volunteer from the audience to play the cat*] The wife whined, the children cried, the dog barked, [*Dog barks*] and the cat meowed. [*Cat meows*]

Who let the cats out?!! [*Storyteller*]
"Meow, meow, meow, meow" [*Audience*]
Who let the cats out?!! [*Storyteller*]
"Meow, meow, meow, meow" [*Audience*]

The man went back to the Rabbi and said, "Rabbi, my life is so miserable. I am in a small house with my wife, our seven children, a barking dog, and a meowing cat. It is always crowded and noisy. What should I do?" The Rabbi said, [*Pause and allow the audience to chime in*]

"It could always be worse!"

Then the Rabbi said, "Get a goose." So the man got a goose. [*Use a volunteer from the audience to play the goose*] The wife whined, the children cried, the dog barked, [*Dog barks*] the cat meowed, [*Cat meows*] and the goose honked. [*Goose honks*]

Who let the geese out?! [*Storyteller*]
"Honk, Honk, Honk, Honk" [*Audience*]
Who let the geese out?! [*Storyteller*]
"Honk, Honk, Honk, Honk" [*Audience*]

The man went back to the Rabbi and said, "Rabbi, my life is so miserable. I am in a small house with my wife, our seven children, a barking dog, a meowing cat, and a honking goose. It is always crowded and noisy. What should I do?" The Rabbi said, [*Pause and allow the audience to chime in*]

"It could always be worse!"

Then the Rabbi said, "Get a goat." So the man got a goat. [*Use a volunteer from the audience to play the goat*] The wife whined, the children cried, the dog barked, [*Dog barks*] the cat meowed, [*Cat meows*] the goose honked, [*Goose honks*] and the goat bleated. [*Goat bleats*]

Who let the goats out?! [*Storyteller*]
"Beeeh, Beeeh, Beeeh, Beeeh" [*Audience*]
Who let the goats out?! [*Storyteller*]
"Beeeh, Beeeh, Beeeh, Beeeh" [*Audience*]

The man went back to the Rabbi and said, "Rabbi, my life is so miserable. I am in a small house with my wife, our seven children, a barking dog, a meowing cat, a honking goose, and a bleating goat. It is always crowded and noisy. What should I do?" The Rabbi said, [*Pause and allow the audience to chime in*]

"It could always be worse!"

Then the Rabbi said, "Get a pig." So the man got a pig. [*Use a volunteer from the audience to play the pig*] The wife whined, the children cried, the dog barked, [*Dog barks*] the cat meowed, [*Cat meows*] the goose honked, [*Goose honks*] the goat bleated, [*Goat bleats*] and the pig oinked. [*Pig oinks*]

Who let the pigs out?! [*Storyteller*]
"Oink, oink, oink, oink" [*Audience*]
Who let the pigs out?! [*Storyteller*]
"Oink, oink, oink, oink" [*Audience*]

The man went back to the Rabbi and said, "Rabbi, my life is so miserable. I am in a small house with my wife, our seven children, a barking dog, a meowing cat, a honking goose, a bleating goat, and an oinking pig. It is always crowded and noisy. What should I do?" The Rabbi said, [*Pause and allow the audience to chime in*]

"It could always be worse!"

Then the Rabbi said, "Get a horse." So the man got a horse. [*Use a volunteer from the audience to play the horse*] The wife whined, the children cried, the dog barked, [*Dog barks*] the cat meowed, [*Cat meows*] the goose honked, [*Goose honks*] the goat bleated, [*Goat bleats*] the pig oinked, [*Pig oinks*] and the horse neighed. [*Horse neighs*]

Who let the horses out?! [*Storyteller*]
"Neigh, neigh, neigh, neigh" [*Audience*]
Who let the horses out?! [*Storyteller*]
"Neigh, neigh, neigh, neigh" [*Audience*]

The man went back to the Rabbi and said, "Rabbi, my life is so miserable. I am in a small house with my wife, our seven children, a barking dog, a meowing cat, a honking goose, a bleating goat, an oinking pig, and a neighing horse. It is always crowded and noisy. What should I do?" The Rabbi said, [*Pause and allow the audience to chime in*]

"It could always be worse!"

Then the Rabbi said, "Get a cow." So the man got a cow. [*Use a volunteer from the audience to play the cow*] The wife whined, the children cried, the dog barked, [*Dog barks*] the cat meowed, [*Cat meows*] the goose honked, [*Goose honks*] the goat bleated, [*Goat bleats*] the pig oinked, [*Pig oinks*] the horse neighed, [*Horse neighs*] and the cow mooed. [*Cow moos*]

Who let the cows out? [*Storyteller*]
"Moo, moo, moo, moo" [*Audience*]
Who let the cows out? [*Storyteller*]
"Moo, moo, moo, moo" [*Audience*]

The man went back to the Rabbi and said, "I can't take it anymore! Rabbi, my life is so miserable. I am in a small house with my wife, our seven children, a barking dog, [*Dog barks*] a meowing cat, a honking goose, a bleating goat, an oinking pig, a neighing horse, and a mooing cow. It is always crowded and noisy. What should I do?" The Rabbi said, [*Pause and allow the audience to chime in*]

"It could always be worse!"

Then the Rabbi said, "Get a job." So the man did. He's now a crossing guard at a school, where it is much quieter. The End.

Jake the Snake

Original

Note from Dianne: *This fun nonsense story is more of a chant or a rap the whole way through. There are fun hand motions. To perform this effectively, the children will echo the first line you sing, along with the hand motions. Once the children learn the rhythm, they often ask to do it again.*

Audience: Grades PK–3, Ages 4–9

Tell along Techniques:

- Repeating chant/song
- Rehearsed response
- Repeating motions

Deep in the grass . . . Swish, swish [*Move hands from side to side*]
There lives a snake . . . Ssss, ssss [*With one hand, make wiggling motions*]
[*Audience participates with storyteller*]
His name is Jake . . . J, J, J, Jake [*Move shoulders up and down with rhythm*]
Jake the Snake . . . Ssss, ssss [*With one hand, make wiggling motions*]

He loves to swim . . . Splash, splash [*Mime swimming*]
Around the lake . . . L, L, L Lake [*Move shoulders up and down with rhythm*]

71

[*Audience participates with storyteller*]
His name is Jake . . . J, J, J, Jake [*Move shoulders up and down with rhythm*]
Jake the Snake . . . Ssss, ssss [*With one hand, make wiggling motions*]

He loves to eat . . . Yum, Yum [*Rub your belly*]
Especially—cake! . . . C, C, C, Cake [*Move shoulders up and down with rhythm*]
[*Audience participates with storyteller*]
His name is Jake . . . J, J, J, Jake [*Move shoulders up and down with rhythm*]
Jake the Snake . . . Ssss, ssss [*With one hand, make wiggling motions*]

He loves to dance . . . Oh yeah [*Do a silly dance move*]
He loves to shake . . . Sh, Sh, Sh, Shake [*Shake shoulders up and down with rhythm*]
[*Audience participates with storyteller*]
His name is Jake . . . J, J, J, Jake [*Move shoulders up and down with rhythm*]
Jake the Snake . . . Ssss, ssss [*With one hand, make wiggling motions*]

He loves to bounce . . . Up and down [*Bounce up and down*]
Like an earthquake . . . Qu, Qu, Qu, Quake [*Move shoulders up and down with rhythm*]
[*Audience participates with storyteller*]
His name is Jake . . . J, J, J, Jake [*Move shoulders up and down with rhythm*]
Jake the Snake . . . Ssss, ssss [*With one hand, make wiggling motions*]

He loves to sleep . . . [*Make snoring sounds*]
When he's not awake . . . W, W, W, Wake [*Move shoulders up and down with rhythm*]
[*Audience participates with storyteller*]
His name is Jake . . . J, J, J, Jake [*Move shoulders up and down with rhythm*]
Jake the Snake . . . Ssss, ssss [*With one hand, make wiggling motions*]

Deep in the grass . . . Swish, swish [*Move hands from side to side*]
There lives a snake . . . Ssss, ssss [*With one hand, make wiggling motions*]
[*Audience participates with storyteller*]
His name is Jake . . . J, J, J, Jake [*Move shoulders up and down with rhythm*]
Jake the Snake . . . Ssss, ssss [*With one hand, make wiggling motions*]

La Petite Fourmi (The Little Ant)

United States

Note from Dianne: *This is a story from Cajun Louisiana. Variants of it can also be found in Mexico and other cultures. It is a cause-and-effect story and has really funny elements (no pun intended). If you are uncomfortable pronouncing the French words, you may eliminate them. Differentiate between the elements by giving them different voices and personalities.*

Audience: Grades 2–6, Ages 7–12

Tell along Techniques:

- Repeating chant/song
- Dramatic pause
- Repeating movement

One day, la petite fourmi, the little ant, was walking.
[*Create and fun and funky tune and dance and have the audience join in, singing with you*]

La la la la la la la la la la la
La la la la la la la la la la la

As she was walking, she slipped on some ice. "Wheeee. Ouch!" La petite fourmi fell on her derriere and began to cry, "Boo hoo hoo." [*Have fun exaggerating the crying*]

Sauterelle, Grasshopper, was walking by when he saw la petite fourmi on the ground. "Why are you crying, mon ami?"

73

La petite fourmi answered, "I slipped on some ice and hurt myself. Now I need some aspirin."

Sauterelle said, "What you really need is justice. You need to find la Neige, the Snow. She froze the water into ice. Ice made you slip and hurt yourself."

La petite fourmi said, "You know what? You're right. Merci beaucoup. Thank you very much."

So la petite fourmi began searching for le Neige, the Snow.

[*Audience to participate with storyteller*]

La la la la la la la la la la la
La la la la la la la la la la la

When la petite fourmi found the Snow, she said, "Snow, I seek justice! You made ice, and ice made me slip and hurt myself."

Snow answered, "It's not my fault. You need to find le Soleil, the Sun. Sun melts me, and he is much stronger than I."

La petite fourmi said, "You know what? You're right. Merci beaucoup. Thank you very much."

So la petite fourmi began searching for le Soleil, the Sun.

[*Audience to participate with storyteller*]

La la la la la la la la la la la
La la la la la la la la la la la

When la petite fourmi found the Sun, she said, "Sun, I seek justice! You melt Snow. Snow makes ice, and ice made me slip and hurt myself."

Sun answered, "It's not my fault. You need to find le Nuage, the Cloud. Cloud covers my face, and he is much stronger than I."

La petite fourmi said, "You know what? You're right. Merci beaucoup. Thank you very much."

So la petite fourmi began searching for le Nuage, the Cloud.

[*Audience to participate with storyteller*]

La la la la la la la la la la la
La la la la la la la la la la la

When la petite fourmi found the Cloud, she said, "Cloud, I seek justice! You cover Sun. Sun melts Snow. Snow makes ice, and ice made me slip and hurt myself."

Cloud answered, "It's not my fault. You need to find le Vent, the Wind. Wind blows me across the sky, and he is much stronger than I."

La petite fourmi said, "You know what? You're right. Merci beaucoup. Thank you very much."

So la petite fourmi began searching for le Vent, the Wind.

[*Audience to participate with storyteller*]

La la la la la la la la la la la
La la la la la la la la la la la

When la petite fourmi found the Wind, she said, "Wind, I seek justice! You blow Cloud. Cloud covers Sun. Sun melts Snow. Snow makes ice, and ice made me slip and hurt myself."

Wind answered, "It's not my fault. You need to find le Mur, the Wall. Wall stops me in my tracks, and he is much stronger than I."

La petite fourmi said, "You know what? You're right. Merci beaucoup. Thank you very much."

So la petite fourmi began searching for le Mur, the Wall.

[*Audience to participate with storyteller*]

La la la la la la la la la la la
La la la la la la la la la la la

When la petite fourmi found the Wall, she said, "Wall, I seek justice! You stop Wind. Wind blows Cloud. Cloud covers Sun. Sun melts Snow. Snow makes ice, and ice made me slip and hurt myself."

Wall answered, "It's not my fault. You need to find Rat. Rat eats a hole right through me, and he is much stronger than I."

La petite fourmi said, "You know what? You're right. Merci beaucoup. Thank you very much."

So la petite fourmi began searching for le Rat, the Rat.

La la la la la la la la la [*Interrupt yourself*]

Suddenly la petite fourmi stopped. "Oh no!" she cried. "Le Rat! Rat eats insects, and I am an . . . INSECT!"

So la petite fourmi decided that it was best to stay away from le Rat. She never did get justice, but at least she didn't get eaten!

[*Audience to participate with storyteller*]

La la la la la la la la la la la
La la la la la la la la la la la

Merci Beaucoup. Thank you very much. [*Take a bow*]

Little Buddy and Old Mother Fox

Old Czechoslovakia

Note from Dianne: *This story is a cautionary tale for children about the dangers of opening the door to strangers. World folklore is filled with tales like these, but I like this version because the fox gets her due in the end and Little Buddy learns a valuable lesson. The little boy's name is originally "Budulinek," but I find that children have a difficult time pronouncing it, so I have simplified it and made him "Little Buddy." Use a sing-songy voice for Old Mother Fox and play up Little Buddy's crying with a lot of exaggerated sniffles. Kids love it and think it's hilarious. It's a lengthy story, but there is enough audience participation to hold children's attention for the 20 minutes it will take to tell this story. There is a lot of repetition, so it is not a difficult story to tell.*

Audience: Grades 1–6, Ages 6–12

Tell along Techniques:

- Audience query

- Repeating chant/song

- Dramatic pause

- Repeating movement

There was once a little boy named Budulinek. His grandmother called him "Little Buddy." Now Little Buddy was the kind of little boy who didn't always listen to his grandmother. Do you know any children like that? [*Direct the question to a grown-up. They will answer yes and laugh.*]

76

Granny had to leave to go to work every day. In the morning she said, "Little Buddy, no matter who knocks, let no one in, especially a fox." Then Granny left Little Buddy with a steaming bowl of porridge and went off to work.

A little while later, there was a knock, knock, knock on the door. [*Mime knocking*]
[*Audience to participate with storyteller*]
"Little Buddy, please let me in
It's Old Mother Fox and I am your friend."
Little Buddy remembered his Granny's warning and said,
[*Audience to participate with storyteller*]
"My Granny said no matter who knocks
Let no one in, especially a fox!"

But Old Mother Fox was clever and knew that little boys loved adventure. She said, "If you let me in without fail, I promise you a ride on my big bushy tail!" [*Wiggle your rear end. The children will laugh.*]

[*Ask the audience directly*] Do you think Little Buddy should open the door? [*The majority of the audience will answer no*] I wish he listened to you but he didn't! Little Buddy opened the door! [*Make a creaking noise*]

Old Mother Fox ran in, headed for the table, and gobbled up all of Little Buddy's porridge. Then she ran back out. Little Buddy had nothing to eat all day, and when Granny came home, he was crying. He said, "I'm hungry!" [*Sniffle, cry and wipe your noise in an exaggerated manner*]

Granny saw that the porridge was gone and asked, "Little Buddy, did you let someone in?"

Little Buddy nodded his head up and down and answered, "Uh huh."

Granny said, "I warned you about letting strangers in! Now I'll make you some more porridge so you don't go to bed hungry." Little Buddy was grateful and hugged his Granny. [*It's funny to single out a grown-up and give them a big hug*]

The next day, Granny had to leave to go to work. She left Little Buddy with a warning and a steaming bowl of peas and went off to work.

A little while later, there was a knock, knock, knock on the door. [*Mime knocking*]
[*Audience to participate with storyteller*]
"Little Buddy, please let me in
It's Old Mother Fox and I am your friend."
Little Buddy remembered his Granny's warning and said,
[*Audience to participate with storyteller*]
"My Granny said no matter who knocks
Let no one in, especially a fox!"

But Old Mother Fox was clever and knew that little boys loved adventure. She said, "If you let me in without fail, I promise you a ride on my big bushy tail!" [*Wiggle your rear end. The children will laugh.*]

[*Ask the audience directly*] Do you think Little Buddy should open the door? [*The majority of the audience will answer no*] He didn't listen to you this time either! Little Buddy opened the door! [*Make a creaking noise*]

Old Mother Fox ran in, headed for the table, and gobbled up all of Little Buddy's peas. Then she ran back out. Little Buddy had nothing to eat all day, and when Granny came home, he was crying. He said, "I'm hungry!" [*Sniffle, cry, and wipe your noise in an exaggerated manner*]

Granny saw that the peas were gone and asked, "Little Buddy, did you let someone in?"

Little Buddy nodded his head up and down and answered, "Uh huh."

Granny said, "I warned you about letting strangers in! Now I'll make you some more peas so you don't go to bed hungry." Little Buddy was grateful and hugged his Granny. [*Single out a different grown-up and give them a big hug*]

The next day, Granny had to go to work again. She left Little Buddy with a warning a steaming bowl of potatoes and went off to work.

A little while later, there was a . . . [*Allow audience to chime in*] knock, knock, knock on the door. [*Mime knocking*]
[*Audience to participate with storyteller*]
"Little Buddy, please let me in
It's Old Mother Fox and I am your friend."
Little Buddy remembered his Granny's warning and said,
[*Audience to participate with storyteller*]
"My Granny said no matter who knocks
Let no one in, especially a fox!"

But Old Mother Fox was clever and knew that little boys loved adventure. She said, "If you let me in without fail, I promise you a ride on my big bushy tail!" [*Wiggle your rear end. The children will laugh.*]

[*Ask the audience directly*] Do you think Little Buddy should open the door? [*The majority of the audience will answer no*] Oh that Little Buddy is foolish. He didn't listen to you again! Little Buddy opened the door! [*Make a creaking noise*]

This time, Old Mother Fox ran in and said, "Climb on my tail, Little Buddy!"

Little Buddy climbed onto Old Mother Fox's big bushy tail. She spun him around and around and around until he was so dizzy he had no idea where he was. Then she dashed home with Little Buddy still riding on her tail.

When Granny came home, Granny saw that Little Buddy was . . . gone! "Oh no! Old Mother Fox has come today and stolen my precious Little Buddy away!" Granny cried and cried.

A little while later, an old man with an organ grinder came by. He cranked his organ grinder and played music. Granny said to the old man, "Old Mother Fox has come today and stolen my precious Little Buddy away! Since you travel so much, could you please keep an eye out for him?"

The old man promised. The next day, as he was traveling through the forest, he heard a little boy crying. He said, "I bet that is Little Buddy!"

He played his organ grinder outside the fox hole:

"Old Mother Fox is dancing a jive
Little Buddy and her foxes, they make five!" [*Hold up five fingers*]

Old Mother Fox said to her oldest child, "Take this penny to the old man and ask him to hush up."

The little fox went outside, and the old man snatched up the fox and stuffed it into the sack.

Once again, he played his organ grinder outside the fox hole:

"Old Mother Fox and two more
Add Little Buddy, he makes four!" [*Hold up four fingers*]

Old Mother Fox said to her second child, "Take this penny to the old man and ask him to hush up."

The little fox went outside, and the old man snatched up the fox and stuffed it into the sack.

Once again, he played his organ grinder outside the fox hole:

"Old Mother Fox and another for me
Add Little Buddy, he makes three!" [*Hold up three fingers*]

Old Mother Fox said to her youngest child, "Take this penny to the old man and ask him to hush up."

The little fox went outside, and the old man snatched up the fox and stuffed it into a sack.

Once again, he played his organ grinder outside the fox hole:

"Old Mother Fox, I'll soon get you
Add Little Buddy, he makes two!" [*Hold up two fingers*]

At last, Old Mother Fox went outside. The old man snatched up Old Mother Fox and stuffed her into the sack with the other three foxes.

The old man played his organ grinder outside the fox hole:

"I've caught those foxes on the run!
Old Mother Fox was the last one!" [*Hold up one finger*]

The old man rescued Little Buddy and returned him to his Granny. From that time on, when there was a knock, knock, knock [*Mime knocking*] on the door, Little Buddy never opened it when he was by himself.

As for Old Mother Fox . . . she never bothered Little Buddy or his family again!

The Little "Read" Hen

Original Adaptation

Note from Dianne: *This is a version of "The Little Red Hen," a folktale from England, that I liberally adapted to simply demonstrate the writing process. I gave it a contemporary twist. It has an interactive refrain that I love to sing with a fun rhythm. Most children are familiar with the story line and those that are not will quickly catch on and participate with gusto.*

Audience: Grades 2–6, Ages 7–12

Tell along Techniques:

- Repeating chant/song
- Dramatic pause
- Movement

Twice as long as long ago, there lived a Little "Read" Hen. She loved to read, and she loved to write! She was an author and needed help with a story. She saw her friends in the coffee shop and asked, "Who will help me research my story?" [*Create a gravelly, chicken-like voice for the Little "Read" Hen. Use this voice for her throughout the story.*]

"Not I," said the Dog.
"Not I," said the Cat.
"Not I," said the Duck.

81

And that was that. [*Create a fun rhythm with this story chorus. You can add a move for each of the animals. You may want to repeat it a couple of times so that the audience catches on to the rhythm and moves.*]

"I'll research it . . . myself," [*Pause after "I'll research it . . ." and point to yourself, emphasizing the word "myself." The audience will catch on and say it with you each time it repeats*] and she did. When she was done searching on Google, poring over articles, and reading reference books, the Little "Read" Hen asked her friends, "Now who will help me write the story?"

"Not I," said the Dog.
"Not I," said the Cat.
"Not I," said the Duck.

And that was that. [*Sing in the fun rhythm. Repeat the animal moves and the audience with join in.*]

"I'll write it . . . myself," [*Pause after "I'll research it . . ." and point to yourself, emphasizing the word "myself." Allow the audience to chime in.*] and she did. When she was done typing the words, placing the paragraphs, and closing her laptop, the Little "Read" Hen asked her friends, "Now who will help me edit the story?"

"Not I," said the Dog.
"Not I," said the Cat.
"Not I," said the Duck.

And that was that. [*Sing in the fun rhythm. Repeat the animal moves and the audience with join in.*]

"I'll edit it . . . myself," and she did. [*Pause after "I'll research it . . ." and point to yourself, emphasizing the word "myself." Allow the audience to chime in.*] When the spelling was checked, the grammar was corrected, and the sentences were rearranged, the Little "Read" Hen asked her friends, "Now who will help me READ the story?"

"I will!" said the Dog.
"I will!" said the Cat.
"I will!" said the Duck.

And that was that. [*Sing in the fun rhythm. Repeat the animal moves and the audience with join in.*]

The Little "Read" Hen said, "Oh, no you won't! No one helped me research the story, edit the story, or write the story. So I'll read it . . . myself!" [*Pause after "I'll research it . . ." and point to yourself, emphasizing the word "myself." All the audience to chime in.*] and she did.

But the Little "Read" Hen found that she was lonely. She realized that a really good story needed to be SHARED. [*Emphasize the word "shared"*] So she found her friends, and they read the story . . . together. [*Pause and give the audience a chance to respond, "to-gether." Most will fill in the blank. If they don't, you can say it with meaning.*]

And you know what? The Little "Read" Hen's friends, the dog, the cat, and the duck LOVED her story. [*Emphasize the word "loved"*] And now they are all "well-read." The end!

The Long-Nosed Princess

Korea

Note from Dianne: *This story is not full of raucous audience participation, although comical elements can be added when the noses grow. The lesson about greed and its consequences is as apparent as the princess's nose. As you repeat the motions of the marble, the flute, and the invisible coat in the story, the audience will catch on and participate with you, even without direct coaching or coaxing.*

Audience: Grades 2–6, Ages 7–12

Tell along Techniques:

- Repeating chant/song

- Dramatic pause

- Repeating movement

Long ago, in the land beyond the stars, there lived an old woman and her three sons. The old woman knew that her days on earth would soon come to an end, so she called her three sons. "I will soon be leaving this earth, but before I do, I want to bestow upon you the family treasures."

The three sons watched as their mother pulled out a small bundle of silk. In it, she had a clear marble, a bamboo flute, and a ragged old coat. [*Mime opening a bundle of silk*]

The oldest son cried out, "These are the family treasures? They are but worthless, ordinary objects!"

The second son said, "Mother, they look like nothing but junk!"

But the third son remained silent, eager to see what his mother had to say. "Sssh, sons. Yes, they do look like ordinary objects, even junk. But the treasure lies beyond what the eyes can see."

She rolled the clear marble across the floor, [*Mime a rolling motion with your hands*] and a trail of gold coins flowed behind it. She played the flute, [*Mime playing a flute*] and a regiment of soldiers appeared, ready to follow orders. She donned the worn coat [*Mime putting on a coat*] and became invisible.

Their mother said, "These treasures are precious, and you must never tell a soul about them for there are many jealous people in this world. Jealousy breeds greed, and greed will snatch your treasures from you."

The old woman gave the marble to her oldest son, [*Mime a rolling motion with your hands*], the flute to her second son, [*Mime playing a flute*], and the worn coat to her youngest son. [*Mime putting on a coat*] Not long after, the old woman closed her eyes for the last time. The three brothers grieved, but their mother left them with lasting gifts.

It didn't take long before the oldest brother began bragging of his great gift. Word reached a selfish princess, and she sent the oldest brother an invitation to show the court his wonderful marble. He was honored and accepted the invitation. Once at the palace, he showed the princess and her court his treasure. A trail of gold coins followed the marble every time he rolled it. [*Mime a rolling motion with your hands*] As it rolled across the floor again, the princess jumped up and snatched it.

[*Invite the audience to say the story chorus with you*]

"Mine, mine, mine! This treasure is mine!
You'll never get it back until the end of time!"

She then sent the young man to the . . . dun, dun, dun . . . [*Create an ominous chant and pause, saying dungeon in a creepy voice*] dungeon!

Like his brother before him, the second brother began bragging of his great gift. Word reached the selfish princess, and she sent the boy an invitation to show the court his wonderful flute. The second brother was honored and accepted the invitation. Once at the palace, he showed the princess and her court his treasure. He said, "When I put this flute to my lips, [*Mime playing a flute*] a regiment of soldiers will appear, ready to take my commands." "Oooh!" squealed the princess. I love it!" The princess jumped up and snatched it.

[*Audience participates with storyteller*]
"Mine, mine, mine! This treasure is mine!
You'll never get it back until the end of time!"

She then sent the young man to the . . . dun, dun, dun . . . [*Create an ominous chant and pause, saying dungeon in a creepy voice*] dungeon!

Days passed, and the youngest boy began to wonder what happened to his brothers. He decided to go to the palace to find out. He put on his magic coat [*Mime putting on a coat*] and, invisible, snuck into the palace without being seen. [*Mime tiptoeing*] He saw the princess in her chamber playing with the marble [*Mime a rolling motion with your hands*] and counting her gold coins. Next to her was the flute. [*Mime playing a flute*]

He carelessly knocked over a table and brushed the princess's leg. She cried out, "Guards, guards! Someone is in my chambers!" As the guards searched, the young boy snuck out of the window in the palace garden. There, he saw an apple tree bearing red and yellow fruit. Feeling hungry, he reached up, grabbed a red apple, and began eating. [*Mime eating an apple*] To his surprise, his nose began to grow!

[*Invite the audience to say the story chorus with you. Mime your nose growing.*]

He had much too much, much too much, much too much nose!
It grew and it grew as long as a hose!

Wondering what he should do, he grabbed a yellow apple and bit it. [*Mime biting an apple*] Before the boy could think, his nose began to shrink. Realizing what a treasure he had, he formulated a plan to help his brothers escape.

The next day, he appeared at the greedy princess's palace with a basket full of red apples.

[*Cup hands around mouth and call out*]

"Apples! Apples! Such a tasty treat!
Who will be the first to bite into this fruit so sweet?"

The princess looked out of her window and said, "I want those apples! Guards, seize those apples!" The guards brought the apples to the princess, and she greedily ate two as fast as she could. To her horror, her nose began to grow!

[*Audience participates with storyteller. Mime your nose growing.*]
She had much too much, much too much, much too much nose!
It grew and it grew as long as a hose!

The youngest brother sprang into action. He put on his magic coat and snuck into the palace again. He found the magic marble [*Mime a rolling motion with your hands*] and flute [*Mime playing a flute*] and took them. Then he searched the dungeons and found his brothers. He unlocked their cells with a key snatched from a sleeping guard.

When the guards realized what happened, they chased the brothers. When the brothers reached the palace gates, the youngest brother blew on the flute, [*Mime playing a flute*] and a regiment of soldiers appeared. The soldiers protected the three brothers as they escaped to safety.

From that time forward, the brothers rejoiced in their gifts and shared them with each other. But they never told another soul about their family treasures.

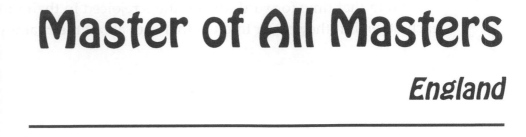

Master of All Masters

England

Note from Dianne: *What makes this story so funny is the kooky language and the hilarious ending. Some of your audience will be scratching their heads, while others will be laughing their heads off. Rattling the ending off very quickly is much more effective. It is a story best used with upper elementary who will be able to decipher the code and understand the humor.*

Audience: Grades 3–6, Ages 8–12

Tell along Techniques:

- Repeating chant/song

- Dramatic pause

- Rehearsed response

There was once a peasant girl who needed to earn some money. So she went looking for a job. At last, a funny old fellow hired her to be his servant.

Her first day on the job, the funny old fellow told her he had many things to teach her because, in his house, he had his own names for things.

He asked her, "What will you call me?"

She answered, "Whatever you like, sir."

He said, "No, that won't do. You must call me 'Master of All Masters.'"

He pointed to a bed. "What would you call this?"

She answered, "Cot or bed, or . . . [*Invite audience to say "whatever you like" with you*] whatever you like."

He said, "No, that's my 'barnacle.'"

He pointed to his pants. "What would you call this?"

She answered, "Pants or trousers, or . . . [*Audience to participate with storyteller*] whatever you like."

He said, "No, these are my 'squibs and crackers.'"

He pointed to his cat. "What would you call her?"

She answered, "Cat or kitten, or . . . [*Audience to participate with storyteller*] whatever you like."

He said, "No, you must call her 'white-faced simminy.'"

He pointed to the fire. "What would you call this?"

She answered, "Fire or flame, or . . . [*Audience to participate with storyteller*] whatever you like."

He said, "No, you must call it 'hot frockadoodle.'"

He pointed to the water. "What would you call this?"

She answered, "Water or wet, or . . . [*Audience to participate with storyteller*] whatever you like."

He said, "No, you must call it 'pondalorum.'"

He pointed to his house. "What would you call this?"

She answered, "House or cottage, or . . . [*Audience to participate with storyteller*] whatever you like."

He said, "No, you must call it 'high topper mountain.'"

That very night the servant woke her master up in a fright and said, "Master of all masters, get out of your barnacle and put on your squibs and crackers. White-faced simminy has a spark of hot frockadoodle on her tail. Unless you get some pondalorum, the entire high topper mountain will be all on hot frockadoodle!"

It's a good thing that servant girl was a quick learner! They splashed some pondalorum on the hot frockadoodle and saved white-faced simminy. And they lived after ever happily!

Medio Pollito (Little Half Chick)

Spain

Note from Dianne: This is a "por quoi" tale or, rather, a "porque" tale since it is from Spain. It is the story of how the weather vane came to be. Many children will not know what a weather vane is, so it is helpful to show them one at end of the story. In Spanish, "Little Half Chick" is known as "Medio Pollito," pronounced MED-ee-oh Poh-YEE-toh. He is a half chick with a full attitude, so have fun with his personality and don't be afraid to exaggerate.

Audience: Grades 1–6, Ages 6–12

Tell along Techniques:

- Repeating chant/song
- Dramatic pause
- Repeating movement

Habia una vez, once upon a time, there was a mother hen who had beautiful little chicks. They were all plump birds except for the youngest. He was different! He had only one wing, one leg, one eye, and half a beak. He was a little half chick, and he was named Medio Pollito.

Although he was just a half chick, he had a full attitude. Mmm hmm! [*Say this with one hand on your hip and do a "chicken" neck move*] He was rough, and he was tough. He wanted to see the king. He'd had enough!

So, against his mother's wishes, he traveled to Madrid to see the king. Nothing was going to get in his way.

90

[*The first time, teach the children the following chant*]

"I'm off to Madrid with a flap and a hop [*Flap your arm and hop on one leg*]
I'm Medio Pollito, and I will not stop!" [*Point to yourself and wave pointer finger from side to side when you say, "I will not stop!"*]

Along the way, he saw a stream choked with weeds. Water cried out, "Medio Pollito, please help me by clearing these weeds." But Medio Pollito refused. He was on his way to see the king. Nothing was going to get in his way.

[*Audience to participate with storyteller*]
"I'm off to Madrid with a flap and a hop [*Flap your arm and hop on one leg*]
I'm Medio Pollito, and I will not stop!" [*Point to yourself and wave pointer finger from side to side when you say, "I will not stop!"*]

By and by, he saw a fire left by some gypsies in the woods. Fire was weak and cried out, "Medio Pollito, please help me by feeding me sticks and leaves." But Medio Pollito refused. He was on his way to see the king. Nothing was going to get in his way.

[*Audience to participate with storyteller*]
"I'm off to Madrid with a flap and a hop [*Flap your arm and hop on one leg*]
I'm Medio Pollito, and I will not stop!" [*Point to yourself and wave pointer finger from side to side when you say, "I will not stop!"*]

A little while later, he saw Wind tangled in the branches of a chestnut tree. The wind cried out, "Medio Pollito, please help me by untangling me." But Medio Pollito refused. He was on his way to see the king. Nothing was going to get in his way.

[*Audience to participate with storyteller*]
"I'm off to Madrid with a flap and a hop [*Flap your arm and hop on one leg*]
"I'm Medio Pollito, and I will not stop!" [*Point to yourself and wave pointer finger from side to side when you say, "I will not stop!"*]

As Medio Pollito approached the king's castle, the king's cook saw him and said, "Just the thing I need for the king's chicken broth!" The cook snatched Medio Pollito and threw him into a pot with water.
Medio Pollito cried, "Water, Water, please help me!"
But Water said, "Medio Pollito, you did not help me when I was a stream choked with weeds. I will not help you."
When Fire began to heat up the water, Medio Pollito cried, "Fire, Fire, please help me!"

But Fire said, "Medio Pollito, you did not help me when I was dying in the woods. I will not help you."

Just as Medio Pollito thought all hope was lost, the cook opened the pot and said, "Oh no! This is but a half chick. This will never do for the king!" The cook threw Medio Pollito out of the window.

Just then, the wind scooped up Medio Pollito. Medio Pollito cried, "Wind, Wind, you've helped me!"

Wind laughed. "Oh no, Medio Pollito. I've come to give you your just punishment for not helping me when I was tangled in the chestnut tree!"

Wind fastened Medio Pollito to the top of the tallest church steeple, where he remains to this day. If you visit Madrid, you can see Medio Pollito perched on the highest church steeple. Medio Pollito became a weather vane.

"I'm on top of a steeple in the middle of town
I'm Medio Pollito and I can't get down!"
El Fin. The End.

Mr. Lucky Straw

Japan

Note from Dianne: *I love this story because it has a chain of good deeds that leads to huge success in the end. This is a great story to tell when you want to illustrate the points of consequences (in this case, good consequences) and serendipity. It is not a long story, so it makes a good filler tale to pull "out of the hat."*

Audience: Grades 1–6, Ages 6–12

Tell along Techniques:

- Repeating chant/song
- Movement

Long ago, there was a young man named Shobei who lived in a farming village in Japan. One day, as he was walking home from the fields, he tripped on a stone and tumbled to the ground. When he stopped rolling, he found a long piece of straw in his hand.

Shobei said, "Since this straw is in my hand, it must be a gift from the land." So he kept it.

As Shobei walked, a dragonfly began circling his head. He said, "What a beauty!" He took the straw and tied it to the dragonfly's tail. [*Mime tying the straw to a dragonfly*]

As Shobei walked, he met a little boy and his mother. The little boy said saw Shobei's dragonfly. It looked like a miniature kite. The little boy asked, "Mother, may I please have that dragonfly? Please, please please!" [*Give the little boy an exaggerated whiney voice*]

93

Shobei said, "Here you go, little boy. This dragonfly will bring you joy." He handed the boy the straw with the dragonfly flying at the end.

The mother was so grateful, she said,
[*Invite the audience to say the story chorus with you*]
"Here is a gift from me to you.
Thank you, thank you for all you do."

She handed Shobei three oranges. Before long, Shobei met a peddler who was thirsty and hungry. Shobei said, "These oranges are quite a treat. Kind old man, please drink and eat." He handed the old man the oranges.

The old man was so grateful, he said,
[*Audience to participate with storyteller*]
"Here is a gift from me to you.
Thank you, thank you for all you do."

He handed Shobei three pieces of cloth. Before long, Shobei met a princess riding in a fine carriage. Shobei thought the princess could use the fabric more than he, so he said, "These three cloths are oh so fine. Princess, they are yours, not mine." He bowed low and presented the fabric to the princess. The princess was delighted.

She was so grateful, she said,
[*Audience to participate with storyteller*]
"Here is a gift from me to you.
Thank you, thank you for all you do."

The princess handed Shobei a big bag of gold. With the gold, he went home and bought three fields. He divided the fields among the people of his village saying,

[*Audience to participate with storyteller*]
"Here is a gift from me to you.
Thank you, thank you for all you do."

The people of Shobei's farming village were very grateful, and everyone benefited from the fruits of their labor. Shobei was honored and respected by everyone. From that time on, Shobei became known as "Mr. Lucky Straw."

The Old Woman and Her Pig

England

Note from Dianne: *This story is a cumulative tale. The simple audience participation makes it perfect for young audiences who will chant and clap with you during the course of the story. If you can speed up your telling as the animals and objects accumulate in the story, it makes it fun for the audience as they try to keep up.*

Audience: Grades PK–3, Ages 4–9

Tell along Techniques:

- Repeating chant/song

- Dramatic pause

- Movement

One evening, an old woman went to market to buy a fat pig. On the way home, she came to a fence. The old woman said, [*Invite the audience to sing the story chorus with you each time it appears in the story*] [*Pause*]

[*Give this a sing-songy Mother Goose type of chant each time you sing it in the story. Audience participates with storyteller.*]
I went to market to buy a fat pig (*Clap, clap*)
Let's go home again—jiggedy jig (*Clap, clap*)

The old woman tried to get her pig to jump the fence, but it wouldn't. She saw a dog and said, [*Pause*]

95

[Audience participates with storyteller]
I went to market to buy a fat pig (*Clap, clap*)
Let's go home again—jiggedy jig (*clap, clap*)

Then the old woman said, "Dog nip the pig. Pig won't jump the fence, and I won't get . . . home tonight!" But the dog would not. She saw a stick and said, *[Pause]*

[Audience participates with storyteller]
I went to market to buy a fat pig (*Clap, clap*)
Let's go home again—jiggedy jig (*Clap, clap*)

Then the old woman said, "Stick, poke the dog. Dog won't nip the pig. Pig won't jump the fence, and I won't get . . . *[Pause and allow audience to chime in]* home tonight!" But the stick would not. She saw a fire and said, *[Pause]*

[Audience participates with storyteller]
I went to market to buy a fat pig (*Clap, clap*)
Let's go home again—jiggedy jig (*Clap, clap*)

Then the old woman said, "Fire, burn the stick. Stick won't poke the dog. Dog won't nip the pig. Pig won't jump the fence, and I won't get . . . *[Pause and allow audience to chime in]* home tonight!" But the fire would not. She saw some water and said, *[Pause]*

[Audience participates with storyteller]
I went to market to buy a fat pig (*Clap, clap*)
Let's go home again—jiggedy jig (*Clap, clap*)

Then the old woman said, "Water, quench the fire. Fire won't burn the stick. Stick won't poke the dog. Dog won't nip the pig. Pig won't jump the fence, and I won't get . . . *[Pause and allow audience to chime in]* home tonight!" But the water would not. She saw an ox and said, *[Pause]*

[Audience participates with storyteller]
I went to market to buy a fat pig (*Clap, clap*)
Let's go home again—jiggedy jig (*Clap, clap*)

Then the old woman said, "Ox, drink the water. Water won't quench the fire. Fire won't burn the stick. Stick won't poke the dog. Dog won't nip the pig. Pig won't jump the fence, and I won't get . . . *[Pause and allow audience to chime in]* home tonight!" But the ox would not. She saw a rope and said, *[Pause]*

[Audience participates with storyteller]
I went to market to buy a fat pig (*Clap, clap*)
Let's go home again—jiggedy jig (*Clap, clap*)

Then the old woman said, "Rope, lasso the ox. Ox won't drink the water. Water won't quench the fire. Fire won't burn the stick. Stick won't poke the dog. Dog won't nip the pig. Pig won't jump the fence, and I won't get . . . *[Pause and allow audience to chime in]* home tonight!" But the rope would not. She saw a rat and said, *[Pause]*

[Audience participates with storyteller]
I went to market to buy a fat pig (*Clap, clap*)
Let's go home again—jiggedy jig (*Clap, clap*)

Then the old woman said, "Rat, gnaw the rope. Rope won't lasso the ox. Ox won't drink the water. Water won't quench the fire. Fire won't burn the stick. Stick won't poke the dog. Dog won't nip the pig. Pig won't jump the fence, and I won't get . . . *[Pause and allow audience to chime in]* home tonight!" But the rope would not. She saw a cat and said, *[Pause]*

[Audience participates with storyteller]
I went to market to buy a fat pig (*Clap, clap*)
Let's go home again—jiggedy jig (*Clap, clap*)

Then the old woman said, "Cat, chase the rat. Rat won't gnaw the rope. Rope won't lasso the ox. Ox won't drink the water. Water won't quench the fire. Fire won't burn the stick. Stick won't poke the dog. Dog won't nip the pig. Pig won't jump the fence, and I won't get . . . *[Pause and allow audience to chime in]* home tonight!" But the cat would not. The cat said, "If you go to the cow and give me milk, I will chase the rat."

So the old woman went to the cow and said, "Please give me some milk." The cow said, "I will give you milk if you go to the barn and get me some hay."

So the old woman went to the barn. Hey! Hey! Hey! She gathered hay!

The old woman gave the hay to the cow. The cow gave her some milk. The old woman gave the milk to the cat. The cat began to chase the rat. The rat began to gnaw the rope. The rope began to lasso the ox. The ox began to drink the water. The water began to quench the fire. The fire began to burn the stick. The stick began to poke the dog. The dog began to nip the pig. The frightened pig jumped over the fence. And that's how the old woman got home that night.

[Audience participates with storyteller]
I went to market to buy a fat pig (*Clap, clap*)
Now I'm home again—jiggedy jig (*Clap, clap*)

The Pilgrims Were Rocking on the Seas

An Original Thanksgiving Tale

Note from Dianne: *This story is more of a chant or a rap the whole way through. There are fun hand motions, and it's a great story to perform in the fall when you are doing lessons on harvest, Thanksgiving, and American Indians. To perform this effectively, the children will echo the first line you sing, along with the hand motions. Once the children learn the rhythm, they often ask to do it again.*

Audience: Grades PK–2, Ages 4–8

Tell along Techniques:

- Repeating chant/song
- Call and response
- Repeating motions

The Mayflower set sail [*Wave both hands up and down to symbolize the ocean*]
The Mayflower set sail [*Audience will repeat storyteller's first line and motions*]
The Pilgrims on the Mayflower set sail

They were rockin on the seas [*Move hands and hips from side to side*]
They were rockin on the seas [*Audience will repeat storyteller's first line and motions*]
The Pilgrims, they were rockin on the seas

98

Then they landed on the rock [*Hold one hand in front of you, palm up. Ball your other hand into a fist and pound it on your open palm.*]
Then they landed on the rock [*Audience will repeat storyteller's first line and motions*]
The Pilgrims landed on Plymouth Rock

It was wintertime [*Hug yourself and make shivering motions*]
It was wintertime [*Audience will repeat storyteller's first line and motions*]
The Pilgrims were cold in the wintertime

Then springtime came [*Hold one arm in front of you horizontally. Slide your other arm up from behind the horizontal arm and open your balled fist. It will look like a flower growing and blossoming.*]
Then springtime came [*Audience will repeat storyteller's first line and motions*]
The Pilgrims were happy when springtime came

They made an Indian friend [*Make the American Sign Language symbol for "friend." Hook your two pointer fingers around each other, placing one pointer on top and then the other.*]
They made an Indian friend [*Audience will repeat storyteller's first line and motions*]
Squanto was the Pilgrim's Indian friend

Squanto helped plant corn [*Make digging motions*]
Squanto helped plant corn [*Audience will repeat storyteller's first line and motions*]
Squanto helped the Pilgrims to plant corn

Then they learned to fish [*Mime casting a fishing line*]
Then they learned to fish [*Audience will repeat storyteller's first line and motions*]
Squanto taught the Pilgrims how to fish

There was plenty of food [*Rub your belly*]
There was plenty of food [*Audience will repeat storyteller's first line and motions*]
The Pilgrims were happy to have plenty of food

So they had a big feast [*Open arms wide*]
So they had a big feast [*Audience will repeat storyteller's first line and motions*]
The Pilgrims and the Indians had a big feast

It was Thanksgiving [*Clap three times, once with each syllable of "Thanksgiving"*]
It was Thanksgiving [*Audience will repeat storyteller's first line and motions*]
Everyone celebrated Thanksgiving! [*Say, "Yay!" and continue clapping*]

Rolling Pancake
Norway

Note from Dianne: *This story is the cousin of "The Gingerbread Man." It is a fun story for directed role playing, where children from the audience can act out the parts of the different animals: chick, hen, rooster, quail, duck, and goose. It is a rollicking, rhythmic story with a lot of movement and participation. If you don't like the pancake being eaten at the end of this story, I have given you an alternate ending.*

Audience: Grades PK–3, Ages 4–9

Tell along Techniques:

- Directed role playing

- Repeating chant/song

- Dramatic pause

- Repeating movement

In a fairy tale kingdom, in a faraway land, in a little village, there lived a mother with seven hungry children. So the mother decided to make a pancake. It bubbled in the butter and fizzled in the fire until it cooked golden brown in the pan.

The mother set the pancake on a plate in the middle of the table. All seven hungry children reached for the pancake at once when suddenly . . . [*Draw out the word "suddenly"*] the pancake rolled away crying,

[*Audience to participate with storyteller*]
"I am Pancake, hot off the pan
I'm rolling away, catch me if you can!"

Everyone just stared open-mouthed as Pancake rolled out the door. The pancake rolled and rolled and rolled [*Roll your hands around as you say, "Rolled and rolled and rolled"*] until it reached a little chick. The little chick called out, "Rolling Pancake, slow down so I can eat you up." But the pancake rolled away crying,

[*Audience to participate with storyteller*]
"I am Pancake, hot off the pan
I'm rolling away, catch me if you can!"

The chick ran after the pancake. The pancake rolled and rolled and rolled [*Roll your hands around as you say, "Rolled and rolled and rolled"*] until it reached a mother hen. The mother hen called out, "Rolling Pancake, slow down so I can eat you up." But the pancake rolled away crying,

[*Audience to participate with storyteller*]
"I am Pancake, hot off the pan
I'm rolling away, catch me if you can!"

The hen ran after the chick, who ran after the pancake. The pancake rolled and rolled and rolled [*Roll your hands around as you say, "Rolled and rolled and rolled"*] until it reached a big rooster. The big rooster called out, "Rolling Pancake, slow down so I can eat you up." But the pancake rolled away crying,

[*Audience to participate with storyteller*]
"I am Pancake, hot off the pan
I'm rolling away, catch me if you can!"

The rooster ran after the hen, who ran after the chick, who ran after the pancake. The pancake rolled and rolled and rolled [*Roll your hands around as you say, "Rolled and rolled and rolled"*] until it reached a small quail. The small quail called out, "Rolling Pancake, slow down so I can eat you up." But the pancake rolled away crying,

[*Audience to participate with storyteller*]
"I am Pancake, hot off the pan
I'm rolling away, catch me if you can!"

The quail ran after the rooster, who ran after the hen, who ran after the chick, who ran after the pancake. The pancake rolled and rolled and rolled [*Roll your hands around as you say, "Rolled and rolled and rolled"*] until it reached a dawdling duck. The dawdling duck called out, "Rolling Pancake, slow down so I can eat you up." But the pancake rolled away crying,

> [*Audience to participate with storyteller*]
> "I am Pancake, hot off the pan
> I'm rolling away, catch me if you can!"

The duck ran after the quail, who ran after the rooster, who ran after the hen, who ran after the chick, who ran after the pancake. The pancake rolled and rolled and rolled [*Roll your hands around as you say, "Rolled and rolled and rolled"*] until it reached a hungry goose. The hungry goose called out, "Rolling Pancake, slow down so I can eat you up." But the pancake rolled away crying,

> [*Audience to participate with storyteller*]
> "I am Pancake, hot off the pan
> I'm rolling away, catch me if you can!"

The goose ran after the duck, who ran after the quail, who ran after the rooster, who ran after the hen, who ran after the chick, who ran after the pancake. The pancake rolled and rolled and rolled [*Roll your hands around as you say, "Rolled and rolled and rolled"*] until it reached the river. There at the river was a . . . FOX. [*Say this in a loud, menacing voice*] Suddenly, the birds stopped and turned the other way. The chick ran after the hen, who ran after the rooster, who ran after the quail, who ran after the duck, who ran after the goose. Seeing the fox, they knew something was afoul!

The rolling pancake was alone with the . . . [*Pause and allow the audience to chime in*] FOX. The rolling pancake said,

> "I am Pancake, hot off the pan
> I can't swim across, help me if you can!"

Fox smiled and said, "Of course!" as he licked his lips. Pancake rolled on top of Fox's snout. Fox said,

"Rolling Pancake, I'm glad you slowed down because now I will eat you up." And he did.

And since the rolling pancake has come to an end, so has this story.

Alternate Ending:

The rolling pancake was alone with the . . . [*Pause and allow the audience to chime in*] FOX. The rolling pancake said,

[*Audience to participate with storyteller*]
"I am Pancake, hot off the pan
I can't swim across, help me if you can!"

Fox smiled and said, "Of course!" as he licked his lips. Pancake rolled on top of Fox's snout. Fox said,
"Rolling Pancake, I'm glad you slowed down because now I will eat you up." But Rolling Pancake hurled himself in the air. He whirled and twirled. He flipped and he flapped. He landed on the opposite bank. He rolled away crying,

"I am Pancake, hot off the pan
And now I'm Flapjack. Catch me if you can!"

So next time you are cooking pancakes, be careful. Rolling Pancake is also an acrobatic Flapjack, who can whirl and twirl and flip and flap through the air. You might never be able to catch him and you too will go . . . hungry!

Sody Sallyraytus

United States

Note from Dianne: *This is one of my most requested, popular tell along tales. This Appalachian mountain tale is reminiscent of "The Three Billy Goats Gruff" because the characters cross a bridge and underneath lives a bear. But he is no ordinary bear! This story is full of boisterous audience participation. Ham it up and give all the characters distinct personalities.*

Audience: Grades K–4, Ages 4–10

Tell along Techniques:

- Repeating chant/song

- Dramatic pause

- Movement

Once there lived a grandpa, [*Make a goofy face for grandpa*] a grandma, [*Mime being an old woman with a cane and no teeth. Children always laugh at this*] a little boy, [*If you want to be bold, pretend to pick your nose. You will elicit surefire laughter and "ewww" from the audience*] a little girl, [*Mime being a prissy little girl*] and their pet squirrel. [*Show buckteeth and wiggle your rear end for the squirrel's tail. You will hear more laughter. This sets the stage for the story*] One day, the grandma wanted to bake some BIG, BEAUTIFUL, BUTTERY [*Emphasize these words*] biscuits, but she was out of sody sallyraytus—baking soda. [*Have the audience repeat "sody sallyraytus" a few times so that they will know how to pronounce it and will repeat it later on in the story. Children love the sound of the word* "sallyraytus."] So she sent the little boy [*Mime the nose picking again*] to the store. He bought the sody and crossed the bridge like this:

Sody sallyratus, lickity-split [*Wave hands from side to side while snapping*]
Grandma's going to bake some biscuits with it. [*Pat hands together as if forming dough*]

Suddenly, out from underneath the bridge appeared a BIG, BAD BULLY BEAR. [*Emphasize each syllable and use a loud voice. Tailor your voice if you have very young children in the audience.*] The big bad bully bear said, "I'm gonna eat you up—you and your sody sallyraytus." He opened his big bear mouth, [*Open your arms wide, like a gator chomping. Ask audience to join in.*] he took a big bear bite, [*Make a chomping sound and simultaneously clap your hands*] and he gobbled the little boy up, just like that. [*Clap your hands three times to each syllable of "just like that"*]

The little boy did not return home, and Grandma said, "That boy is taking too long!" So she sent the little girl [*Mime the prissy girl*] to the store. The little girl bought the sody and crossed the bridge like this:

Sody sallyratus, lickity-split [*Wave hands from side to side while snapping*]
Grandma's going to bake some biscuits with it. [*Pat hands together as if forming dough*]

Suddenly, out from underneath the bridge appeared a BIG, BAD BULLY BEAR. [*Emphasize each syllable and use a loud voice*] The big bad bully bear said, "I ate the little boy. Now I'm gonna eat you up—you and your sody sallyraytus." He opened his big bear mouth, [*Open your arms wide, like a gator chomping. Audience will join in.*] he took a big bear bite, [*Make a chomping sound and simultaneously clap your hands*] and he gobbled the little girl up, just like that. [*Clap your hands three times to each syllable of "just like that"*]

The little girl did not return home and Grandma said, "That girl is taking too long!" So she sent Grandpa [*Make the goofy face*] to the store. Grandpa bought the sody and crossed the bridge like this:

Sody sallyratus, lickity-split [*Wave hands from side to side while snapping*]
Grandma's going to bake some biscuits with it. [*Pat hands together as if forming dough*]

Suddenly, out from underneath the bridge appeared a BIG, BAD BULLY BEAR. [*Emphasize each syllable and use a loud voice*] The big bad bully bear said, "I ate the little boy. I ate the little girl. Now I'm gonna eat you up—you and your sody sallyraytus." He opened his big bear mouth, [*Open your arms wide, like a gator chomping. Audience will join in.*] he took a big bear bite, [*Make a chomping sound and simultaneously clap your hands*] and he gobbled Grandpa up, just like that. [*Clap your hands three times to each syllable of "just like that"*]

Grandpa did not return home, and Grandma said, "That old man is taking too long! I'll fetch it myself." So she went to the store. She bought the sody and crossed the bridge like this:

Sody sallyratus, lickity-split [*Wave hands from side to side while snapping*]
Grandma's going to bake some biscuits with it. [*Pat hands together as if forming dough*]

Suddenly, out from underneath the bridge appeared a BIG, BAD BULLY BEAR. [*Emphasize each syllable and use a loud voice*] The big bad bully bear said, "I ate the little boy. I ate the little girl. I ate the old man. Now I'm gonna eat you up—you and your sody sallyraytus." He opened his big bear mouth, [*Open your arms wide, like a gator chomping. Audience will join in.*] he took a big bear bite, [*Make a chomping sound and simultaneously clap your hands*] and he gobbled Grandpa up, just like that. [*Clap your hands three times to each syllable of "just like that"*]

Now the pet squirrel was home by himself getting hungrier and hungrier. He went to the store. The storekeeper said the little boy, the little girl, the grandpa, and the grandma had all been there to buy . . . sody sallyraytus. [*Allow audience to chime in "sody sallyraytus"*] So the squirrel started home and crossed the bridge like this:

Sody sallyratus, lickity-split [*Wave hands from side to side while snapping*]
Grandma's going to bake some biscuits with it. [*Pat hands together as if forming dough*]

Suddenly, out from underneath the bridge appeared a BIG, BAD BULLY BEAR. [*Emphasize each syllable and use a loud voice*] The big bad bully bear said, "I ate the little boy. I ate the little girl. I ate the old man. I ate the old woman. Now I'm gonna eat you up—you and your sody sallyraytus."

"Oh no you won't!" [*Stick out your tongue and blow a raspberry*] said the little squirrel, and lickity-split, he ran up a nearby tree. The big, bad bully bear began climbing that tree and following the squirrel. He growled, "If you can do it with your little legs, then I can do it with my big legs!"

But the branch could not bear the big, bad bully bear and it broke. Dooooooww-wwn he fell. THUD! Well, that bear fell so hard that out bounced the little boy, the little girl, Grandma, and Grandpa. And out bounced four boxes of . . . sody sallyraytus.

[*Allow audience to chime in "sody sallyraytus"*] They started home and crossed the bridge, just like this:

Sody Sallyraytus, lickity split
Grandma's going to bake some biscuits with it.

And she did. She made some BIG, BEAUTIFUL, BUTTERY [*Emphasize these words*] biscuits. They all opened their hungry mouths, [*Open your arms wide, like a gator chomping. Audience will join in*] they took a big hungry bite, [*Make a chomping sound and simultaneously clap your hands*] and they gobbled those biscuits up, just like that. [*Clap your hands three times to each syllable of "just like that"*]
The squirrel sang:

Mmm, mmm, mmm
Yummy in my tummy
The biscuits Grandma made us
From . . . sody sallyraytus [*Allow audience to chime in "sody sallyraytus"*]

The Three Little Girls

Korea

Note from Dianne: You will notice familiar elements in this story. It is a combination of both a cautionary tale (stranger danger) and a pour quoi tale (how and why). A portion of this story will remind you of the classic "Little Red Riding Hood." I did not change the girls' names because those names become very important at the end of the story.

Audience: Grades 2–6, Ages 7–12

Tell along Techniques:

- Repeating chant/song

- Movement

- Dramatic pause

Deep in the mountains, there stood a lonely little hut. In this hut lived a mother and her three lovely daughters, Haisuni, Talsuni, and Peolsuni.

One day, the mother had to go to town to sell firewood at the market. Before she left she said, "Be careful and watch out for danger. Don't open the door to any stranger." She kissed Haisuni, Talsuni, and Peolsuni good-bye.

Just as the mother left, a big bad tiger passed by the house. He was . . . [*Rub your belly and allow audience to chime in*] hungry! The tiger said, "Now that their mother is gone, I am going to have me a fine meal!"

He disguised himself and knocked on the door.
[*Invite audience to say the story chorus with you*]
"Mother is knocking, 1, 2, 3 [*Mime knocking*]
Open the door just for me."

The eldest child, Haisuni, asked, "Is that you, Mother? What a gruff voice you have."
The tiger answered, "I was singing at a feast. That is why my voice is gruff."

The tiger knocked on the door again.
[*Audience to participate with storyteller*]
"Mother is knocking, 1, 2, 3 [*Mime knocking*]
Open the door just for me."

The second child, Talsuni, asked, "Is that you, Mother? What red eyes you have."
The tiger answered, "I was grinding pepper pods. That is why my eyes are so red."

The tiger knocked on the door again.
[*Audience to participate with storyteller*]
"Mother is knocking, 1, 2, 3 [*Mime knocking*]
Open the door just for me."

The youngest child, Peolsuni, asked, "Is that you, Mother? What yellow hands you have."
The tiger answered, "I was helping our neighbors plaster their house with mustard mud. That is why my hands are so yellow."
The tiger fooled the girls and the youngest girl opened the door for their mother. But it was not their mother! It was a big bad . . . [*Allow audience to chime in*] tiger! The tiger said, "Mother is going to fix you a nice dinner!" He began boiling water in a big pot.
The girls knew what the tiger was up to. He was . . . [*Rub your belly and allow audience to chime in*] hungry! He planned to eat them up so they ran out of the house and hid at the top of a nearby tree.
The tiger realized that Haisuni, Talsuni, and Peolsuni were gone. He found them in the tree and called out,

[*Have audience say with you*]
"How oh how do I climb this tree?"
Haisuni answered, "Rub sesame oil on the trunk."
The tiger did and, of course, the trunk was too slippery to climb up.

He called out again,

[*Audience to participate with storyteller*]
"How oh how do I climb this tree?"
Talsuni answered, "Rub coconut oil on the trunk."
The tiger did and, of course, the trunk was too slippery to climb up.

He called out again,
[*Audience to participate with storyteller*]
"How oh how do I climb this tree?"
Peolsuni the youngest, not thinking, answered, "Use an ax to cut notches in the tree trunk. Then you can climb up."

The tiger did and, of course, he climbed up the tree trunk. He almost reached the girls when Haisuni prayed to Heaven for a bucket. Her prayers were answered, and a bucket at the end of a golden rope appeared. The girls climbed in and were carried away into the sky.

The three little girls were given special tasks to keep the sky bright with light. Haisuni shone during the day, Talsuni glowed at night, and Peolsuni twinkled between them. To this day in Korea, the sun is called Haisuni, the moon is called Talsuni, and the stars are called Peolsuni.

As for that big bad tiger, he still sulks to this day about the dinner that got away!

Tio Rabbit and the Barrel

Panama

Note from Dianne: *This is a story about a clever rabbit. In Spanish, "Tio" means "Uncle," but in this story, "Tio" is more akin to "Brother" or "Brer" as in the "Brer Rabbit" tales of the American South. I love how Tio Rabbit outsmarts the animals who are trying to eat him up. There is a lot of fun audience participation in this story.*

Audience: Grades K–4, Ages 5–10

Tell along Techniques:

- Repeating chant/song

- Repeating motions

Un dia, one day, Tio Rabbit was hippity-hopping down the road to journey to his abuela, his grandma's, house. Suddenly, Tio Jaguar jumped in front of Tio Rabbit growling,
[*Invite audience to say story chorus with you*]

"I want to eat a rabbit, big and fat [*Move hands out from stomach, signaling "fat"*] I'm going to eat you up, just like that!" [*Clap three times during "just like that," one clap for each syllable*]

Tio Rabbit said,
[*Invite audience to say story chorus with you*]

111

"Tio Tio Jaguar, please don't eat me [*Wave one pointer finger from side to side, signaling "don't"*]

I'll get fat at abuela's, wait and see!" [*Move hands out from stomach, signaling "fat," then put one hand above your eye as if you are looking*]

So Tio Jaguar said, "Alright. I'll eat you up when you come back."

Tio Rabbit continued hippity-hopping down the road to journey to his abuela's house. Suddenly, Tio Lion jumped in front of Tio Rabbit growling,

[*Audience participates with storyteller*]

"I want to eat a rabbit, big and fat [*Move hands out from stomach, signaling "fat"*]

I'm going to eat you up, just like that!" [*Clap three times during "just like that," one clap for each syllable*]

Tio Rabbit said,

[*Audience participates with storyteller*]

"Tio Tio Lion, please don't eat me [*Wave one pointer finger from side to side, signaling "don't"*]

I'll get fat at abuela's, wait and see!" [*Move hands out from stomach, signaling "fat," then put one hand above your eye as if you are looking*]

So Tio Lion said, "Alright. I'll eat you up when you come back."

Tio Rabbit continued hippity-hopping down the road to journey to his abuela's house. Suddenly, Tio Fox jumped in front of Tio Rabbit growling,

[*Audience participates with storyteller*]

"I want to eat a rabbit, big and fat [*Move hands out from stomach, signaling "fat"*]

I'm going to eat you up, just like that!" [*Clap three times during "just like that," one clap for each syllable*]

Tio Rabbit said,

[*Audience participates with storyteller*]

"Tio Tio Fox, please don't eat me [*Wave one pointer finger from side to side, signaling "don't"*]

I'll get fat at abuela's, wait and see!" [*Move hands out from stomach, signaling "fat," then put one hand above your eye as if you are looking*]

So Tio Fox said, "Alright. I'll eat you up when you come back."

When Tio Rabbit arrived at his abuela's house, his abuela fed him carrots, cabbage, lettuce, radishes, and watermelon. Soon, he was three times as fat as when he arrived!

After a month with his abuela, Tio Rabbit was ready to go home. He hugged his grandmother adios and hippity-hopped down the road.

When he was out of his abuela's sight, he found a barrel and climbed inside. Down the hill, Tio Rabbit rolled. He hadn't rolled far when he came across Tio Jaguar. Tio Jaguar asked, "Little Barrel, have you seen Tio Rabbit?"

Inside the barrel, Tio Rabbit disguised his voice and said,
[*Audience participates with storyteller*]

"Run, Tio Jaguar, the forest's on fire
Tio Rabbit is burned and I'm not a liar."

Tio Jaguar became scared and ran away, believing that the forest was on fire. Down the hill, Tio Rabbit rolled. He hadn't rolled far when he came across Tio Lion. Tio Lion asked, 'Little Barrel, have you seen Tio Rabbit?"

Inside the barrel, Tio Rabbit disguised his voice and said,
[*Audience participates with storyteller*]

"Run, Tio Lion, the forest's on fire
Tio Rabbit is burned and I'm not a liar."

Like Tio Jaguar, Tio Lion became scared and ran away, believing that the forest was on fire. Down the hill, Tio Rabbit rolled. He hadn't rolled far when he came across Tio Fox. Tio Fox asked, "Little Barrel, have you seen Tio Rabbit?"

Inside the barrel, Tio Rabbit disguised his voice and said,
[*Audience participates with storyteller*]

"Run, Tio Fox, the forest's on fire
Tio Rabbit is burned and I'm not a liar."

But Tio Fox was not fooled. He recognized Tio Rabbit's voice and said, "Little Barrel, you are a liar. You are Tio Rabbit and I'm going to eat you up!" But down the hill, Tio Rabbit rolled. Tio Fox chased after the barrel but it rolled farther and farther away. Tio Fox was out of breath and gave up.

Tio Fox heard Tio Rabbit's voice in the distance,

"I'm a clever rabbit, big and fat [*Move hands out from stomach, signaling "fat"*]
And I got away, just like that!" [*Clap three times during "just like that," one clap for each syllable*]

The Travels of a Fox

England

Note from Dianne: *This is an old English nursery tale. The sly old fox knows that each time he asks the lady of the house not to open the bag, she will, leaving him to the larger spoils. In the end, of course, the fox gets his due. You will see this motif repeated time and again in folktales where one animal is eaten by another animal (think "I Know an Old Lady Who Swallowed a Fly"). This story is not about the food chain (oxen do not eat pigs, and pigs do not eat roosters). It is about how deceit is foiled in the end. The repetitious pattern will allow children to anticipate and predict what will happen next.*

Audience: Grades 1–4, Ages 6–10

Tell along Techniques:

- Repeating chant/song

- Dramatic pause

One day, a fox was digging behind a stump when he found a bumblebee. He put the bumblebee in his sack and traveled. At the first house he came to, he asked the lady of the house,

[Invite the audience to say the story chorus with you]
"I'm going to Squintum's. May I leave my sack?
Don't open it up until I get back."

114

The lady agreed, but as soon as the fox left, she became curious. She opened the sack, and the bumblebee flew out. The rooster caught him and . . . gobbled him up.

When the fox returned, he saw that his bumblebee was gone. The lady said, "I opened the sack, and the rooster . . . [*Pause to let the audience chime in*] gobbled him up."

The fox said, "Very well. Then I must have the rooster." He put the rooster in his sack and traveled.

At the next house he came to, he asked the lady of the house,

[*Audience participates with storyteller*]
"I'm going to Squintum's. May I leave my sack?
Don't open it up until I get back."

The lady agreed, but as soon as the fox left, she became curious. She opened the sack, and the rooster ran out. The pig caught him and . . . [*Pause to let the audience chime in*] gobbled him up.

When the fox returned, he saw that his rooster was gone. The lady said, "I opened the sack, and the pig . . . [*Pause to let the audience chime in*] gobbled him up."

The fox said, "Very well. Then I must have the pig." He put the pig in his sack and traveled.

At the next house he came to, he asked the lady of the house,

[*Audience participates with storyteller*]
"I'm going to Squintum's. May I leave my sack?
Don't open it up until I get back."

The lady agreed, but as soon as the fox left, she became curious. She opened the sack, and the pig ran out. The ox caught him and . . . [*Pause to let the audience chime in*] gobbled him up.

When the fox returned, he saw that his pig was gone. The lady said, "I opened the sack, and the ox . . . [*Pause to let the audience chime in*] gobbled him up."

The fox said, "Very well. Then I must have the ox." He put the ox in his sack and traveled.

At the next house he came to, he asked the lady of the house,

[*Audience participates with storyteller*]
"I'm going to Squintum's. May I leave my sack?
Don't open it up until I get back."

The lady agreed, but as soon as the fox left, she became curious. She opened the sack, and the ox ran out. Her little boy chased the ox out the door.

When the fox returned, he saw that his ox was gone. The lady said, "I opened the sack, and my little boy chased him out the door."

The fox said, "Very well. Then I must have the little boy." He put the little boy in his sack and traveled.

At the next house he came to, he asked the lady of the house,

[*Audience participates with storyteller*]
"I'm going to Squintum's. May I leave my sack?
Don't open it up until I get back."

The lady agreed and pulled a cake out of the oven. Her children began begging for a piece. The delicious smell of the cake drifted inside the sack, and the little boy inside began whimpering, "Mammy, please give me some cake too."

The lady opened the sack and let the little boy out. She put the dog in the little boy's place. A bit later, the fox returned. He took his sack and traveled.

After a while, the fox started to get hungry. He said, "This little boy will make a tasty treat! I'm so hungry, I can't wait to eat!"

He opened the sack and the dog ran out. The dog caught the fox and . . . [*Pause to let the audience chime in*] gobbled him up. And that was the end of the fox's travels!

Source Notes

"Anansi Shares Wisdom with the World" was adapted from "Anansi Tries to Gain Wisdom" in *Around the World in 80 Tales* by Nicola Baxter (Leicester: Bookmart Limited, 2002) and *Anansi Gives Wisdom to the World* by Patricia C. McKissack (Des Moines, IA: Hampton-Brown, 2007) and "Anansi Tries to Steal All the Wisdom in the World" on the Wisdom Commons website at http://www.wisdomcommons.org/virtue/135-wisdom/parables.

"Anansi's Hat Shaking Dance" was adapted from "Anansi's Hat-Shaking Dance" in *The Arbuthnot Anthology of Children's Literature, Third Edition*, edited by May Hill Arbuthnot (Glenview, IL: Scott, Foresman and Company, 1952) and "Anansi's Hat-Shaking Dance" in *Best-Loved Folktales of the World*, edited by Joanna Cole (New York: Anchor Books by Doubleday, 1982).

"Bag of Truth, The," was adapted from "The Bag of Truth" in *Stories from Spain* by Edward W. Dolch and Marguerite P. Dolch (Champaign, IL: Garrard Publishing Company, 1962).

"Bobtail Monkey, The," was adapted from "The Bobtail Monkey" in *Japanese Children's Favorite Stories* (Rutland, VT: Charles E. Tuttle Company, 1958).

"Bremen Town Musicians, The," was adapted from "The Four Musicians" in *The Arbuthnot Anthology of Children's Literature, Third Edition*, edited by May Hill Arbuthnot (Glenview, IL: Scott, Foresman and Company, 1952); "The Bremen Town Musicians" in *The Complete Fairy Tales of the Brothers Grimm*, edited by Jack Zipes (New York: Bantam Books, 1987); "The Bremen Town Musicians" in *Best-Loved Folktales of the World*, edited by Joanna Cole (New York: Anchor Books by Doubleday, 1982); and "The Bremen Town Musicians" in *The Dial Book of Animal Tales* by Naomi Adler (New York: Dial Books for Young Readers, 1996).

"Elephant and Snake" was adapted from "One Cold Day in Louisiana" in *With a Whoop and a Holler* by Nancy Van Laan (New York: Atheneum Books for Young Readers, 1998) and "Elephant and Serpent" in *Cajun and Creole Folktales*, collected and edited by Barry Jean Ancelet (Jackson: University Press of Mississippi, 1994).

"Fortunately, Unfortunately" is an original story based on an improvisation word play game where players create the story as they go, switching between "fortunately" and "unfortunately." There is a book called *Fortunately* by Remy Charlip (New York: Aladdin, 1993) that chronicles the adventures of a boy named Ned, who tries to get to a party. It follows the same pattern as the "Good News, Bad News" or "Oh, That's Good! No, That's Bad" types of stories.

"Golden Goose, The," was adapted from "The Golden Goose" in *The Complete Fairy Tales of the Brothers Grimm* by Jack Zipes (New York: Bantam Books, 1987); *The Golden Goose* by Dennis McDermott (New York: Morrow Junior Books, 2000); "The Golden Goose" in *Best-Loved*

Folktales of the World, edited by Joanna Cole (New York: Anchor Books by Doubleday, 1982); and "The Golden Goose" on the Grimms Fairy Tale at All Family Resources website at http://www.familymanagement.com/literacy/grimms/grimms50.html.

"Gourd of Honey, The," was adapted from "Uncle Bouqui and Godfather Malice" in *The Arbuthnot Anthology of Children's Literature, Third Edition,* edited by May Hill Arbuthnot (Glenview, IL: Scott, Foresman and Company, 1952); "The Theft of Honey" in *Cajun Folktales* by J. J. Reneaux (Little Rock, AR: August House, 1992); and "Uncle Bouqui and Little Malice" in *Best-Loved Folktales of the World,* edited by Joanna Cole (New York: Anchor Books by Doubleday, 1982).

"It Could Always Be Worse!" was adapted from *It Could Always Be Worse* by Margot Zemach (New York: Farrar, Straus and Giroux, 1976); "It Could Always Be Worse" in *Best-Loved Folktales of the World,* edited by Joanna Cole (New York: Anchor Books by Doubleday, 1982); and *Too Much Noise* by Ann McGovern (New York: Houghton Mifflin Company, 1992).

"Jake the Snake" is an original story chant I crafted as a nonsensical, fun story.

"La Petit Fourmi" was adapted from "Neige Casse La Patte de la Froumi" in *Cajun and Creole Folktales,* edited by Barry Jean Ancelet (Jackson: University Press of Mississippi, 1994), and "La Hormiguita" in *Multicultural Folktales: Stories to Tell Young Children* by Judy Sierra and Robert Kaminski (Phoenix, AZ: Oryx Press, 1991).

"Little Buddy and Old Mother Fox" was adapted from "Budulinek" in *The Arbuthnot Anthology of Children's Literature, Third Edition,* edited by May Hill Arbuthnot (Glenview, IL: Scott, Foresman and Company, 1961), and "Budulinek" from The Baldwin Project website at http://www.mainlesson.com/display.php?author=lmr&book=k2rainbow&story=budulinek.

"Little 'Read' Hen, The," was adapted from "The Little Red Hen" from childhood memories of the story; "The Little Red Hen and the Grain of Wheat" in *Story Time of My Bookhouse,* edited by Olive Beaupré Miller (Lake Bluff, IL: The Book House for Children, 1965); and "Little Red Hen and the Grains of Wheat" in *Troll Treasury of Animal Stories,* edited by John C. Miles (Mahwah, NJ: HarperCollins, 1991).

"Long-Nosed Princess, The," was adapted from *Too Much Nose: An Italian Tale* by Harve Zemach (New York: Reader's Digest Services, 1967); "The Long-Nosed Princess" in *Korean Folk-Tales* retold by James Riordan (Oxford: Oxford University Press, 1994); and *The Greedy Princess* adapted by Duance Vorhees & Mark Mueller (Elizabeth, NJ: Hollym International Corp., 1990).

"Master of All Masters" was adapted from "Master of All Masters" in *The Everything Fairy Tales Book* by Amy Peters (Avon, MA: F+W Publications, 2001) and "Master of All Masters" in *Best-Loved Folktales of the World* edited by Joanna Cole (New York: Anchor Books by Doubleday, 1982).

"Medio Pollito" was adapted from "The Half-Chick" in *The Arbuthnot Anthology of Children's Literature, Third Edition,* edited by May Hill Arbuthnot (Glenview, IL: Scott, Foresman and Company, 1961); "The Half-Chick" in *Best-Loved Folktales of the World,* edited by Joanna Cole (New York: Anchor Books by Doubleday, 1982); and "Medio Pollito" by Eric A. Kimmel (Tarrytown, NY: Marshall Cavendish, 2010).

"Mr. Lucky Straw" was adapted from "Mr. Lucky Straw" in *Japanese Children's Favorite Stories* (Rutland, VT: Charles E. Tuttle Company, 1958) and *Mr. Lucky Straw* by Elizabeth Lane (Salt Lake City, UT: Electronic Education, 2003).

"Old Woman and Her Pig, The," was adapted from "The Old Woman and Her Pig" in *English Fairy Tales* by Joseph Jacobs (New York: Alfred A. Knopf, 1993 [first published in 1890]); "The Old Woman and Her Pig" in *The Arbuthnot Anthology of Children's Literature, Third Edition,* edited by May Hill Arbuthnot (Glenview, IL: Scott, Foresman and Company, 1961); and "The Old Woman and Her Pig" in *Troll Treasury of Animal Stories,* edited by John C. Miles (Mahwah, NJ: Troll Associates, 1991).

"Pilgrims Were Rocking on the Seas, The," is an original story chant I wrote to give young children an easy way to understand the first Thanksgiving. I based the time line on the book *The First Thanksgiving* by Jean Craighead George (New York: Philomel Books, 1993).

"Rolling Pancake" was adapted from "The Pancake" in *The Arbuthnot Anthology of Children's Literature, Third Edition,* edited by May Hill Arbuthnot (Glenview, IL: Scott, Foresman and Company, 1961), and *The Pancake That Ran Away* by Loek Koopmans (Edinburgh: Floris Books, 1992).

"Sody Sallyraytus" was adapted from "Sody Sallyraytus" in *Grandfather Tales*, collected and retold by Richard Chase (Cambridge, MA: The Riverside Press, 1948), and "Sody Saleratus" in *Crocodile! Crocodile! Stories Told Around the World* by Barbara Baumgartner (New York: Dorling Kindersley Publishing, 1994).

"Three Little Girls, The," was adapted from "The Three Little Girls" in *Korean Children's Favorite Stories* by Kim So-un (Rutland, VT: Tuttle Publishing, 1955) and "The Sun, The Moon, and The Stars" in *Korean Folktales* retold by James Riordan (Oxford: Oxford University Press, 1994).

"Tio Rabbit and the Barrel" was adapted from "Tio Rabbit and the Barrel" in *Tales from Around the World* by Graham Percy (New York: Barnes & Noble Books, 2003) and "Tio Rabbit and the Barrel" in *The Enchanted Orchard and Other Folktales of Central America* by Dorothy Sharp Carter (New York: Harcourt, 1973).

"Travels of a Fox, The," was adapted from "The Travels of a Fox" in *The Arbuthnot Anthology of Children's Literature, Third Edition,* edited by May Hill Arbuthnot (Glenview, IL: Scott, Foresman and Company, 1961); "The Travels of a Fox" in *Multicultural Folktales: Stories to Tell Young Children* by Judy Sierra and Robert Kaminski (Phoenix, AZ: Oryx Press, 1991); and "The Travels of a Fox" from The Baldwin Project website at http://www.mainlesson.com/display.php?author=lmr&book=k2rainbow&story=travels.

Web Resources

Besides the books I have listed in my Source Notes, these are great Web resources.

Call of Story

Through the Eccles Foundation, this website was developed to bring awareness to story-telling. Watch videos that feature several nationally known tellers, including Donald Davis, Rex Ellis, and Carmen Deedy.
http://www.callofstory.org

Doug Lipman, Storytelling Coach

Doug Lipman is the leading storytelling coach in the country. His books and work-shops on coaching and the art of storytelling have inspired thousands of storytellers. Doug provides many useful articles on his website.
http://www.storydynamics.com

Story-Lovers.com

This is Jackie Baldwin's site. Her company, Story-Lovers, produces gorgeous stationery using illustrations from old folktales and children's stories. Jackie generously provides a free service to storytellers called SOS—Searching Out Stories. Here, you can find lists of stories and story resources pertaining to many different topics. There is a section on audience participation and fantastic sections on traditional folktale openings and clos-ings. Jackie also produces *Bare Bones* booklets, with bare bones of stories from around the world. Story-Lovers.com is a gold mine of information.
http://www.story-lovers.com

Sean Buvala's Storyteller.net

Sean has been on the Web since 1996, providing storytellers with a great service through his website. He offers a storyteller directory, articles, interviews with storytellers, and

free stories. In addition, he offers storytelling resources on his site. Storyteller.net is a treasure trove for storytellers.
http://www.storyteller.net

Storytelling Power

Storytellingpower.com is, in my opinion, one of the most useful storytelling resource websites on the internet. Chris King, creator of the site, writes extremely helpful articles on all aspects of storytelling. Don't miss this one.
http://www.storytellingpower.com

Tim and Leanne Jennings's Folktale Openings and Closings

Tim and Leanne have graciously compiled an extensive collection of traditional folktale openings and closings.
http://www.folktale.net

Creative Diversity

Creative Diversity is a great company that has "multicultural products for early childhood." I love their basket of instruments from around the globe.
http://www.hatchearlychildhood.com/subcategory.asp?cn=Creative%20
Diversity&scn=Instruments%20(CD)

Storyboard Worksheet

I love this storyboard worksheet. It can be used when you are creating your own tellable tales.
http://www.eduplace.com/rdg/gen_act/pigs/story_mp.html

Recommended Reading

Baltuck, Naomi. *Crazy Gibberish and Other Story Hour Stretches*. Linnet Books, 1993.

Baltuck, Naomi. *Apples from Heaven: Multicultural Folk Tales about Stories and Storytellers*. Linnet Books, 1995.

Baltuck, Naomi. *Storytime Stretchers: Tongue Twisters, Choruses, Games and Charades*. August House, 2007.

Bauer, Caroline Feller. *New Handbook for Storytellers*. ALA Editions, 1995.

Birch, Carol. *The Whole Story Handbook: Using Imagery to Complete the Story Experience*. August House, 2000.

Birch, Carol, and Melissa Heckler. *Who Says? Essays on Pivotal Issues in Contemporary Storytelling*. August House, 1996.

Bronner, Simon. *American Children's Folklore: A Book of Rhymes, Games, Jokes, Stories, Secret Languages, Beliefs and Camp Legends*. August House, 1988.

Bruchac, Joseph. *Tell Me a Tale: A Book about Storytelling*. Harcourt Brace, 1997.

Cole, Joanna. *Best-Loved Folktales of the World*. Doubleday, 1982.

DeSpain, Pleasant. *Thirty-Three Multicultural Tales to Tell*. August House, 1997.

Forest, Heather. *Wonder Tales from Around the World*. August House, 1998.

Fujita, Hiroko, and Fran Stallings. *Stories to Play With: Kids' Tales Told with Puppets, Paper, Toys, and Imagination*. August House, 1999.

Greene, Ellin. *Storytelling: Art and Technique*, 3rd ed. Libraries Unlimited, 1996.

Harrison, Annette. *Easy-to-Tell Stories for Young Children*. National Storytelling Press, 1992.

Haven, Kendall. *Super Simple Storytelling: A Can-Do Guide for Every Classroom, Every Day*. Libraries Unlimited, 2000.

Haven, Kendall, and Mary Gay Ducy. *Crash Course in Storytelling*. Libraries Unlimited, 2006.

Holt, David, and Bill Mooney. *Ready-to-Tell Tales: Sure-Fire Stories from America's Favorite Storytellers*. August House, 1994.

Holt, David, and Bill Mooney. *More Ready-to-Tell Tales from Around the World*. August House, 2000.

Huff, Mary Jo. *Storytelling with Puppets, Props and Playful Tales*. Monday Morning Books, 1998.

Lipman, Doug. *The Storytelling Coach: How to Listen, Praise, and Bring Out People's Best*. August House, 1995.

Lipman, Doug. *Storytelling Games: Creative Activities for Language, Communication and Composition across the Curriculum*. Oryx Press, 1995.

Livo, Norma, Teresa Miller, and Anne Pellowski. *Joining In: An Anthology of Audience Participation Stories and How to Tell Them*. Yellow Moon Press, 1988.

MacDonald, Margaret Read. *The Storyteller's Sourcebook: A Subject, Title, and Motif Index to Folklore Collections for Children*. Gale Research, 1982.

MacDonald, Margaret Read. *Twenty Tellable Tales: Audience Participation Folktales for the Beginning Storyteller*. H. W. Wilson, 1991.

MacDonald, Margaret Read. *The Storyteller's Start-Up Book: Finding, Learning, Performing, and Using Folktales: Including Twelve Tellable Tales*. August House, 1993.

MacDonald, Margaret Read. *Shake-It-Up Tales! Stories to Sing, Dance, Drum, and Act Out*. August House, 2000.

MacDonald, Margaret Read. *The Parents' Guide to Storytelling: How to Make Up New Stories and Retell Old Favorites*. August House, 2001.

MacDonald, Margaret Read. *The Storyteller's Sourcebook: A Subject, Title, and Motif Index to Folklore Collections for Children (2002 Supplement)*. Gale Research, 2002.

MacDonald, Margaret Read. *Tell the World: Storytelling across Language Barriers*. Libraries Unlimited, 2008.

Maguire, Jack. *Creative Storytelling: Choosing, Inventing, and Sharing Tales for Children*. McGraw-Hill, 1985.

National Storytelling Network. *A Beginner's Guide to Storytelling*. National Storytelling Press, 2003.

National Storytelling Network. *Telling Stories to Children*. National Storytelling Press, 2005.

Pellowski, Anne. *The Storytelling Handbook: A Young People's Collection of Unusual Tales and Helpful Hints on How to Tell Them*. Simon and Schuster, 1995.

Pellowski, Anne. *Drawing Tales from Around the World and a Sampling of European Handkerchief Tales*. Libraries Unlimited, 2005.

Seeger, Pete, and Paul Jacobs. *Pete Seeger's Storytelling Book*. Harcourt, 2000.

Sherman, Josepha. *Trickster Tales: Forty Folk Stories from Around the World*. August House, 1996.

Stotter, Ruth. *About Story: Writings on Stories and Storytelling 1980–1994*. Stotter Press, 1996.

Stotter, Ruth. *More about Story: Writings on Stories and Storytelling 1995–2001*. Speaking Out Press, 2002.

Yolen, Jane. *Favorite Folktales from Around the World*. Pantheon Books, 1986.

About the Author and Illustrator

DIANNE DE LAS CASAS is an award-winning author and story-teller who tours internationally presenting programs, educator/librarian training, workshops, and artist residencies. Her performances, dubbed "revved-up storytelling" are full of energetic audience participation. Dianne's professional books include *Handmade Tales: Stories to Make and Take; Tangram Tales: Story Theater Using the Ancient Chinese Puzzle, The Story Biz Handbook, Scared Silly: 25 Tales to Tickle and Thrill, Stories on Board: Creating Board Games from Favorite Tales, Tell Along Tales: Playing with Participation Stories, A is for Alligator: Draw and Tell Tales from A-Z,* and *Tales from the 7,000 Isles: Filipino Folk Stories.* Her children's books include *The Cajun Cornbread Boy, Madame Poulet & Monsieur Roach, Mama's Bayou, The Gigantic Sweet Potato,* and *There's a Dragon in the Library.* Visit her website at www.storyconnection.net.

SOLEIL LISETTE is a graphic design student at Louisiana State University in Baton Rouge. Since she was two years old, she could always be found with a pen in her hand—drawing! Her career aspirations include illustrating children's books and beginning her own line of cosmetics. When not at school, Soleil lives in the New Orleans area. Visit Soleil's website at www.soleil-lisette.com.

CPSIA information can be obtained at www.ICGtesting.com
Printed in the USA
LVOW011450260313

326143LV00012B/300/P